ANGELS, DIVAS AND
BLACKLISTED HEROES

Jeremy Reed

ANGELS, DIVAS AND BLACKLISTED HEROES

Peter Owen
London and Chester Springs

Peter Owen Publishers
73 Kenway Road, London SW5 0RE

Peter Owen books are distributed in the USA by Dufour Editions, Inc.,
Chester Springs, PA, 19425-0007

First published in Great Britain 1999
© Jeremy Reed 1999

A catalogue record for this book is available from the British Library

ISBN 0 7206 1052 4

Printed and bound in Great Britain by Hillman Printers (Frome) Ltd

'Gender in Genet's Poetry' was first published as a booklet by Joe Di Maggio
Press; 'Saint Oscar' and 'The Angel in Poetry' were delivered as talks to the
Temenos Academy and 'The Angel in Poetry' was published by the Temenos
Academy as a limited edition booklet; 'Strange Sister' appears in the anthology
Montale tradotto dai poeti; 'A Hundred Years of Disappearance' was published as a
booklet by Alan Clodd; the essay on 'Soul Inside' was a limited edition booklet
by Silk Excursion and that on 'L'Esqualita' first appeared in the Marc Almond
fanzine *Obsession*; 'Endgaming' was first published in *Entropy*.

For Karl Orend,
John Robinson and Lene Rasmussen

PREFACE

Over the years, and in the main thrust of my creative expression through writing poetry, fiction and non-fiction, the dynamic which has preoccupied me most has been that of the committed imagination. By this I mean the inspired celebration of the weird, the wild and the wonderful. I have always believed in an art that takes risks and challenges complacency with the apprehension of the imaginatively marvellous.

The essays that make up this volume are a cocktail of homogenous obsessions. If my overriding concerns in literature have been with outsiders like Jean Genet and the Comte de Lautréamont (about whom I wrote a novel called *Isidore*) then I have applied a corresponding passion in life to their counterparts in music. My love of torch singers, both male and female, instanced here by studies of Marc Almond, Scott Walker and Billie Holiday, is a devotion inseparable from my love of poetry. The perfect phrasing, the dramatic innuendos and the essentially life-affirming energies at work in the heart of a torch singer's repertoire should go to sensitize the poetic faculty. When Frank Sinatra advised 'keeping the whole thought of the song in mind' while singing it, he was only paraphrasing what has, for centuries, been the poetic principle.

The group of artists I have chosen to write about here are also linked by the common theme of commitment; that is, they have made their life their art. Creativity, if is it to ring true, demands an acquisition of experience which is in itself a lifetime's occupation. To me the idea of the part-time poet lacks authenticity and conviction. This book is equally about those who have suffered for their art, not in a pejorative way but in a manner that has contributed to its triumphant summation. It was William Blake who wrote that 'Eternity is in love with the productions of Time', and, while Scott Walker is able to read Lautréamont and Marc Almond Oscar Wilde, one would wish that the reverse was possible too and that the dead writers could listen to singers with whom they would have found much common territory.

But is that not the point of writing – to make felicitous intersections between the living and the dead and to achieve this through empathy with both distinctions? I could call this collection *A Little Book of Heroes*.

I have always believed that a torch burns at the top of the stairs.

Jeremy Reed

CONTENTS

1 Gender in Genet's Poetry 11

2 Poe, Opium and the Pathology of the House of Usher 23

3 Saint Oscar 43

4 Strange Sister 67

5 The Angel in Poetry 79

6 A Hundred Years of Disappearance: Count Eric Stenbock 109

7 Poetry, Madness and Masturbation 117

8 Heroic Gestures: Scott Walker, Frank Sinatra, Marc Almond 137

9 Reflections: 'Soul Inside' and 'L'Esqualita' 153

10 Engaming: Scott Walker's *Tilt* 163

Further Reading and Listening 175

A Diva a day
Keeps the boredom away
I love it when they throw up their arms.

Marc Almond, 'St Judy'

We'll let this life burn out, no matter how.

Thomas Lovell Beddoes, *The Bride's Tragedy*

GENDER IN GENET'S POETRY

IN the photograph of Jean Genet I keep on my writing table, he
stands contemplatively with his back to the Seine, his eyes
focused on Philippe Halsman who is out of the picture. It is 1951,
and Genet is forty. He's informally dressed in a white cotton
shirt, open at the neck, a suede zipper jacket and jeans. All of his
defiance, vulnerability and deeply wounded poetic sensibility are
concentrated into Halsman's shot. You can't hear the traffic in a
photograph, but you can imagine the audial backdrop to a late
afternoon in Paris. Genet is not only looking at the camera but
also at the configurative poem he carries in his head. The poet's
preoccupation with an unconscious archetypal text, and its externalization through bits of autonomous imagery, invests the person
with an air of distraction. Poets are distracted by virtue of biloca-
tion and their inhabiting parallel worlds. Inner and outer realities,
unconscious and conscious states are differentiated but unified by
the poetic line. The image is the big now, the immediate, the
mythopoetic arrival. As Jung tells us: 'Image and meaning are
identical; and as the first takes shape, so the latter becomes clear.'

Genet's poetry, as opposed to the prose poems he called novels,
belongs to the high-octane imaginative tradition of Baudelaire,

Lautréamont and Rimbaud. It was Rimbaud who propagated the notion of the poet as *voyant*, inspired visionary and, pertinent to Genet, as the great criminal or social outcast. The poet lives in a metaphoric desert. He is an exile, the one who refuses to be demystified by ideologies and who inhabits an imaginal universe. The sand in a poet's shoes turns to gold.

Genet's dictum that 'poetry is the art of using shit and making you eat it' may be seen as iconoclastically subversive or simply alchemical in its coprophilic reference. Genet's inversion of all moral precepts, and most principally his exclusion of women from the uniformly homoerotic microcosm of his poetics, instates a world of psychophysical gender substitutes. In an interview with Madeleine Gobeil in 1964 Genet commented: 'Homosexuality was imposed on me like the colour of my eyes or the number of my feet. Even when I was still a child I was conscious of being attracted by other boys I have never felt desire for women.'

In Genet's poetry gender transference, or in his terms 'a refusal to continue the world', involves not only altering sexuality but implies subscribing to a passive attitude, one in which the adoption of feminine characteristics suggests sexual sterility rather than the manifestation of a failed woman. Genet equates the unregenerative qualities of homosexuality with his lengthy periods of creative impotence. He is blocked by his inability to become his fluent opposite. In Genet's first literary creation, the poem 'The Man Sentenced to Death', which he published at his own expense while imprisoned in Fresnes during 1942, he evokes the androgynous blueprint for his later intensely lyrical and homoerotic novels. His masturbatory ideal, envisaged as a tough blond kid, is equally transposable into the feminine role of a princess in a tower. Genet writes:

> Don't sing Bullies of the Moon tonight.
> Blond-haired kid, be a princess in a tower
> introspectively dreaming of our love
> or a tight-jeaned cabin-boy up on deck.

While the poem is dedicated to Maurice Pilorge, a murderer who, Genet claims, was executed at the age of twenty, it also represents the romantic idealization of a gay fraternity and the celebration of an invincible thug who will be the self-appointed King of the Underworld. Within the formal structure of rhymed alexandrine quatrains, Genet pitches a subversive sexual current against his constraining form. In what is in fact a paean to fellatio, Genet instigates a conflict between romantic diction and criminal slang and in the process succeeds in criminalizing poetry. And it's not so much that the poem consciously excludes women, it's more that Genet writes as if they don't exist. Genet's prototypical thugs double for women because there are no other options. His poetics recreate the universe, and they do so by imaginatively transforming gender. Genet's problems are not so different from de Sade's on a physiological plane. He would like to reconstruct anatomy and find in his felt-androgyny a corresponding physical completion. A new species, but one generated without the mediating force of women. Genet's poetic universe is at all times fantastic, surreal and structured out of the mythopoetic contents of the unconscious. Genet saw the role of the poet as mediumistic. The poet makes himself especially receptive to occult and irrational forces which exist independent of the intellect. The visionary poet is set apart by this difference; his life is spent waiting and listening for the voice to come through. The aural desert is constelled by images. The poet catches them like falling stars.

'The author of a beautiful poem is always dead,' Genet tells us in *Miracle of the Rose*, and Genet's overriding sense of a dead childhood, which can only be redeemed by poetry, was one of the psychological determinants of his creative impulse. Rimbaud's belief in the poet making himself a seer through an inner programme involving 'the systematic derangement of the senses' finds a corresponding practice in Genet's liberal use of amphetamines while writing and in the belief that the poet animates the explosive force situated in objects or things. Genet makes his lovers into poems, in the sense that the word inseminates myth and it gives tangible form to an ideal which had previously existed only in the imagination. For Genet, poetry is like masturbation; it embodies the fantastic through concentrated manipulation of the image. Genet's characters exist only through his creating them as constructs within the poem. They are exact replications of his sexual fantasies. The poet is omnipotent in this sense: he has absolute power over a subjective state. And so it is that Genet invents his murderers, queens, pimps and boys who are transposable to girls. In 'The Man Sentenced to Death' he celebrates his conception of the immutable legendary hero who was to become the prototype for his novels:

> Let's dream together, love, of a hoodlum
> big as the universe, body splashed with tattoos.
> He'll strip us, lock us into bondage cells,
> and show us how between his golden thighs
> and on his smoking stomach, a hot pimp
> works it up on carnations and jasmine.

Genet had begun work on *Our Lady of the Flowers* at this time and the poem and the novel share a corresponding lyric thrust. The explicit homoeroticism in both works, the opulent poetic diction contrasting a classic literary language with prison slang, and the uninhibited dynamic behind the celebration of taboo, invested Genet's work with a sense of individuated and scandalous genius. Genet's mythologems had been externalized as seething jewels. They studded his work with the fascinating glitter of poetic evil. They sat on the page like sapphires or black rubies.

In *The Thief's Journal* Genet professes how the wound or the death he experienced in childhood had him seek to narrate his life as a legend or to subjectify living until the experience became in itself the poem: 'I refuse to live for any other end but that contained by the wound. My life must be a legend, or legible, and the reading of it must give birth to a particular new emotion which I call poetry.'

Genet's insistence on transforming the ordinary into the legendary, and in constantly inventing a life for himself, make all of his biographical statements appear suspect. Poetry substitutes imaginative truth for reality, it hypostatizes the moment in a way that has the poet lie in the act of revealing truth. The intended contents of the poem are altered by the fiction of writing it. The poet becomes the magician, the word-thief, the image conjuror, and language, in its mediating between inner and outer realities, establishes, at best, a meta-truth.

Where do we look for Genet? In the poem or outside of it? His grizzled head, small figure, suffering eyes, his inveterate leather jackets, his sartorial oscillation between dandy and thug, his image as international writer and scandalous criminal, all the tension and discord in his conflicting personae make Genet into one of the most concealed of writers. Not even Edmund White's exhaustively researched and superbly eloquent biography succeeds in bringing Genet out into the light. He evades exposure.

There's a sharp, realistic taste of the man in Mohamed Choukri's pithily minimal *Jean Genet in Tangier*, a book that catches Genet at a certain time in a certain place and evokes the natural angularity and perversely hostile presentation of his views on life, politics and literature. The real Genet is essentially in his poetry, in the romantic and celebratory impulse behind a self-created world, one over which he presides by the directed psychic energies of the imagination. In his poem 'The Fisherman from Suquet' Genet creates the object of his desire, and the writing of the poem is the extension of libido: 'A gold dust floats around him, and keeps him at a remove.' This boy could be anyone, but he is apotheosized in the process of being created by Genet: 'A complicity, a consent are established between my mouth and the cock – still concealed in his blue shorts – of this eighteen-year-old fisherman.' The desire for fellatio becomes the poem's entry point. 'The Fisherman from Suquet' has themes in common with Hart Crane's marine sequence, *Voyages*, in which love and death are celebrated through tidal flux and the exotic imagery of drowned sailors and sub-aquatic cities. Genet's imaginary love is both compliant and resistant to his advances; the autonomous contradictory energies that inform the poem also connect with the tensions that govern a real relationship. But more often the legend overtakes:

> I wade into love as one does the sea,
> palms first, blinded, my grief
> holding back to keep your presence alive,
> you're heavy, eternal, and I love you.

Genet is similar to Rimbaud in that he makes the subjective conflict of writing poetry the subject of the poem. Imaginative conception cries out on the line. It is blood, fire, tears and anguish, an emotional arena in which the poet risks everything for a charged inner reality. The qualitative power of that truth is assembled through imagery which is in turn the vocabulary of psyche.

In keeping with Genet's instinctual attraction to the androgyne, the masculine image in 'The Fisherman from Suquet' is reused as part of Genet's need to unify opposites within gender. He becomes she while remaining he: 'But he's melting in my mouth. Only one verse. For which girl and what garden? What dream makes him drowsy, tumbles him into himself, delicately torments him, and twists his stomach in anticipation.'

In an undated letter to Sartre, probably written in 1952, which Edmund White quotes in full in *Genet*, Genet attempts to struggle against the pessimistic feelings of sterility that he associates with homosexuality. Writing, for him, represented transcendence over the sexual nihil, an activation of 'funereal themes in the imagination'. The act becomes the writing of the poem and the latter itself is seen as a generative symbol. He writes as a postscript to his letter to Sartre: 'A poem is only the activity of a funereal theme. It is (definitely) its socialization, a struggle against death. The themes of life propose action and forbid the poem.' And so it is that Genet lives inside the poem and dies within life. Most of his lifelong anomie and passive resignation to suffering were occasioned by his increasing inability to write. Without the inspirational act of poetry Genet squandered life. In his post-prison years the magic of a closed, homoerotic ethos denied him; he seems never again to have found the same creative centre to his life. An increasing addiction to Nembutal which acted as a downer to his neurophysiology, his unfocused peripatetic life, his quasi-affiliation to revolutionary political causes; most of Genet's later life was a distraction from his dead creative energies. In fact, as early as 1950, that is after the writing of *The Thief's Journal*, Genet seems to have been disinherited from the poem. If prison symbolized a metaphoric castle from which he wrote, separated from society, then his eviction from that site left him exposed to liberty, and all the diversity, diffuseness and chaos implied by that state. Given freedom, Genet became imprisoned by creative sterility. It was as though he had left his genius on the inside and was unable to recreate that phenomenon in the social world.

It's in his poem 'A Love Song' that Genet gives most eloquent expression to the excessively sensual voice by which he recreates gender. Nowhere is the poem more interchangeable with the imaginatively created body of the lover. The poem makes itself available to be fucked, and in a very real sense Genet is observed writing the poem with his penis. Sexual and psychic energies are orchestrated into a singular dynamic. The poem explodes at orgasmic pitch. It detonates with romantic longing for the impossible love:

> From blood on stones or an open wound
> who will be born, what page-boy or angel of ivy
> will choke me? What soldier wearing your dead nails?

Genet sees himself 'naked on a blue staircase' and foundering in a dream. The poet fights to externalize the poem. He is terrified of his vision collapsing and of being unable to sustain the tension between subjective and objective universes: 'Tired of dying on the brink of my lips/the horizon fell asleep in your folded arms.'

Everything will close down if the poet loses breath. His imaginal, and by extension physical, universe will black out. Genet assumes deistic responsibility for the poem. It exists because of him; the whole psychophysical infrastructure of its organism rests on his energized thrust to sustain inspiration. If the poem runs out on the poet, or the poet deserts his source, then the continuity of creation is interrupted. The Big Bang short-fuses. In the context this poet is a star-thrower, one who constellates and extends a continuous galaxy. Writing poetry means lighting up the world. Throwing a switch to the stars. Everything jumps into place.

Nor does the intense, white-hot fever of homoerotism in Genet's poetry preclude heterosexual interest. All love is one love if it's fired by passionate sensuality. 'How I love any kind of love,' Marc Almond sings in his composition 'There Is a Bed'. 'A Love Song' is shot through with unrelieved gender confusion:

> In his torso, asleep, and cream-coloured
> like an almond, a little girl lies coiled,
> blood tinkles along the blue avenue
> and evening stamps a bare foot on the lawn.

Here the instance of androgyny is not only psychically visualized but also physically realized. The feminine is envisaged as curled like a foetus in the male torso. Genet, who professed contempt for fags and drag queens and who idealized straight-looking lovers, nevertheless writes a poetry of androgynous consciousness and often dresses his syntax in drag. A Genet sentence is heavy with rhinestones. Out on the street it attracts attention to itself and is in trouble. Genet writes of 'a thief's five fingers with carmine nails'.

There's a breathtaking lyrical beauty to Genet's poetry, a hauntingly ambiguous quality to his search for islands, undiscovered paradises, apolitical utopias and legendary states which invests it with a visionary luminosity. In the tradition of Lautréamont, Rimbaud and Saint-John Perse, Genet sets out to discover the subject of the poem in the course of writing it. Lyric impulse becomes the experiential meaning of the poem. And there are times when Genet sounds like the Perse of *Amers*:

> But the green flag of the sea wanderers
> has to keep watch somewhere, stretched between poles.
> Shake the blue night, powder your shoulders with it,
> drill air columns into your sandy feet.

One of the dominant features of Genet's work is his deface-ment of beauty, his subversion of the underlying dynamic to his work. Genet fears to look on beauty; he can only imagine it. His fear of demystifying the world of things has him turn inward to a world of psychic autonomy. He tells us something of this excruci-ating paradox in *The Thief's Journal*:

> I dared not even look at the beauty of that part of the world – unless it
> were to look for the secret of that beauty, the imposture behind it, to
> which one falls a victim of trust. By rejecting it, I discovered poetry.

By rejecting Andalusia he recreates it through poetry. It is a country made real through the externalization of the contents of the poet's psyche. An Andalusia which is a sounding-board of the poet's organism.

There will always be two kinds of poetry. One which turns inwards and recreates the universe through imaginative transfor-mation and another which is concerned purely with observing and experiencing objective phenomena: the Dionysian and Apollonian, unconscious and conscious energy channels. Genet belongs to the tradition of poets who amaze us by their discovery of a transcendental quality in the ordinary. The poet either heightens or debases reality and through the substitution of metaphor for observed phenomena stands back from a world he has created through image-mythopoetics. You walk down the same road every day and suddenly it's a highway to the stars. Everything observed becomes something else in the transformative flash. The poet closes his eyes and dreams of freedom. Genet does this in 'The Man Sentenced to Death':

> O, the sweetness of impossible islands,
>
> delusional skies, the sea and the palms,
>
> transparent mornings, mad evenings, calm nights,
>
> heads that are shaved, and satin skins.

Something of Genet's need to make poetry into a subversive raid on the established order of things, a psychological impulse not so dissimilar from theft, is expressed in his attitude to Hitler's Germany in *The Thief's Journal*. Granted the freedom to commit crime, Genet found himself impotent to steal. 'If I steal here, I perform no singular act that might appease me. I obey the customary order; I do not destroy it. I'm not committing evil. I'm not disturbing anything. The outrageous is prevented me. I'm stealing in the void.'

And so it is with his poetry. The anarchic opposition to civilization is the drive behind lyric impulse. And in the process gender is also re-evaluated and rearranged. The imagination is the weapon with which the poet violates hierarchies. It is also the liberator from passivity. It breaks down pre-existent orders and imposes unconditional freedom; a freedom which extends to everything, including gender.

I began with a photograph. The picture will never change. Genet was different before the moment in which Halsman isolated him against the backdrop of the Seine. He was different for the remaining thirty-five years of his life. But in that instant he has become a frozen image. It's an afternoon in Paris. His books are behind him but he doesn't know it. Nobody knows him. He can slip anonymously back to the bookstalls along the *quais* and browse, drift with the afternoon, telephone a friend, arrange a rendezvous at a bar. He's in the same process of becoming as he was at the moment of his death.

POE, OPIUM AND THE PATHOLOGY OF THE HOUSE OF USHER

WANT to fast-forward in Poe's biography to September–October 1849. A man in a crumpled black suit, wearing neither a shirt nor tie, his clothes moulded to his skin by the torrential autumn rain, is sitting in Gunner's Hall, a bar in Baltimore. In fact, it is 3 October 1849 to the factitious; but to Poe time has become the fiction he has spent a lifetime creating. Sitting in the bar, incoherent, his hallucinations when they are voiced indicate delirium tremens. He is sweating profusely and visibly in distress. He is disconnected from the language fired in his direction. He is apparently without money or identity, he who has afforded identity to so many fictitious characters, and is dissociated from environment. Wherever he is situated in consciousness it isn't comfortable.

People don't react well to those who are manifesting symptoms of mental distress in public. Henry Herring, Poe's uncle by marriage, has been called for and there's an acquaintance of his from Philadelphia in town, but neither men own to any responsibility for the demented vagrant. And, as with all disturbance, the subject has involuntarily grown to be the focus of attention. People are now staring. The stranger has activated the fear within them that they, too, could go mad. He has already reached that place by a long and terrible descent, and the derealizing effects of alcohol have contributed to his psychic crash.

After a period of concentrated time, in which Poe is objectified by the company, it is decided among them that he should be hospitalized. He is still in sporadic dialogue with his hallucinations as they drive him through the blinding rain to the hospital at Washington Medical College. The imposing building has vaulted Gothic windows and could by freak associations be considered to have escaped from the metaphysical architectonics of Poe's mind. Part of Poe's disintegration is characterized by his fiction becoming reality. With his inner defences collapsed, he is powerless to prevent a confrontation with the external equivalents of his shadow.

Still phased and partly amnesiac, Poe is admitted to the care of Dr John J. Moran, who works on the ward for alcoholics. Poe has some advantage in that Dr Moran is aware of his notoriety as a writer and of his patient's highly individual sensibility. He is conscious that the shivering, wrecked individual in his charge has always experienced problems with reality. Poe is unaware of who or what has brought him to this ward and is immediately given sedation. Dr Moran is a witness to what he later describes as Poe addressing 'spectral and imaginary objects on the walls'. In the course of the next day Poe is alternately confused and violently delirious, and when he does make contact with his doctor it is to complain of the degradation of his position. Poe expresses feelings of humiliation and asks his doctor to blow his brains out. His dypsomaniacal ravings are punctuated by suicidal impulses, and Poe is kept under the scrutiny of two nurses. He remains in a confused state for another day, repeatedly calling out an incomprehensible name, and then, exhausted from his exertions, expires. He is forty years old. It is still raining.

Medical cause of death: encephalitis. Inflammation of the brain brought on by exposure. It is suggested that the drunken and inadequately dressed Poe contracted fever while shuttling from bar to bar in the city.

In the course of his writing life Poe had invented a great number of possible deaths for himself. The psychological extremes of his imagination had invested in a pathological empathy with death-states initiated by mental terror. Poe's situation of death is never within the conceivably natural. His devitalized characters are created to undergo deaths that are invariably sensational. And all of these fictions or splinter-deaths appear to be organized around the author's apprehension of the possible circumstances that would attend his own eventual demise.

Poe's life was outwardly controversial. He married Virginia Clemm, who he called 'Siss', when she was thirteen, the secret marriage in Baltimore being legitimized the following year in Virginia. He was lionized as a critic for his uncompromising severity, attractive to women for his black-suited stage presence when lecturing, infamous for his reckless consumption of alcohol, considered insane by his contemporaries and was himself the creator of an endlessly sustained self-legend. Poe was the proto-type of today's pop stars haloed by press rumours of drug and drink scandals.

It takes a time before I dare write the name Roderick Usher. Of all Poe's psychological studies, or reinventions of himself, Usher and his sister Madeline are the most formidably modern. They belong to the repertoire of nervous manias and obsessions that asserted a compulsive fascination over Poe. Like most poets, Poe identified with madness but hoped never to experience it. He lived his life with the idea of psychosis but avoided its reality in as much as he controlled delusional states by writing. Roderick Usher can be taken as the model for how Poe conceived of himself as mad, should he have crossed that frontier.

The traveller, who in Poe's story arrives at the House of Usher at the time of autumn dissolution and melancholy, is of course the author's investigative faculty inquiring at the house of madness. The scene that the arrival views is so charged with terror that he can compare it 'to no earthly sensation more properly than to the afterdream of the reveller upon opium'. It will be noticed how Poe immediately transposes the Gothic accoutrements associated with the brooding house and its decaying trees to a comparison with altered states of consciousness. The narrator questions his vision: 'What was it – I paused to think – what was it that so unnerved me in the contemplation of the House of Usher?'

The psychological answer, independent of the narrative suspense that the author is in the process of establishing, is possibly that Poe has recognized a space in which to situate his madness. He has established that place as separate from reality. The house finds its reflection in a 'black and lurid tarn' and there's every reason to read the pool as a symbol for the archetypal structure of Poe's unconscious.

It is within this disquieting 'mansion' that the narrator proposes to spend a number of weeks with his old school friend Roderick Usher. Usher has complained in a letter of 'a mental disorder which oppressed him', and this first indication of a radically disordered psychology is Poe's cue to elaborate on the disturbed condition of his subject. We are told that the years have transformed the already vitiated Roderick Usher into a state of physical and nervous decay paralleled by the gradual ruin of the house in which he lives. The mirroring process of inner and outer will run throughout the story and by this means increase the scale of terror that Poe is always in danger of overstating. His imagination works in terms of extreme contrasts. He will have all or nothing for his plot.

The vaulted room in which the narrator finds the derealized Roderick Usher is, in its depiction, Poe's ideal for a theatre of madness. The high windows admit almost no light, and in Poe's description:

> Dark draperies hung upon the walls. The general furniture was profuse, comfortless, antique and tattered. Many books and musical instruments lay scattered about, but failed to give any vitality to the scene. I felt that I breathed an atmosphere of sorrow. An air of stern, deep, and irredeemable gloom hung over and pervaded all.

Poe's introduction to the mental precinct in which he imagines his madness to exist is through a vaulted door to a Gothic interior. Today we would imagine Usher in his lowlight room, listening to sampled tape loops, with portraits of Nick Cave and William Burroughs firmed to the walls.

Poe's full description of Usher is of someone invalided by nervous illness. Roderick's bleached-out features, the luminous distraction of his eye, his wild and fuzzily managed hair and his voice range modulating between tremulousness and grave assertion all suggest somebody encountering inner crisis; the sort of crisis that Poe periodically announced in letters to be his own. Poe, who had difficulty in differentiating between imagination and reality, has Usher obsessively fixated by his sister's cataleptic symptoms. His sister Madeline is suffering from a rare condition by which she is presumed medically dead but each time pronounced so returns to life. This notion of being buried alive was a compulsive neurosis of Poe's and one shared in common with his contemporaries, which, while it is rooted in Gothic literature, is afforded additional terror by Poe's exploitation of its worst psychological aspects. What it is like to encounter this unnatural state is observed through Roderick's mania rather than through Madeline's realization of her illness. Poe's method is to see how far he dare imagine the prospects of premature burial and then to push it further. In a letter to William Evans Burton, Poe had hinted at his removal from the ordinary. Commenting on the latter's bad review of his *Narrative of Gordon Pym* he had written: 'In a general view of human nature your idea is just – but you will find yourself puzzled in judging me by ordinary motives.'

'Usher' is an extraordinary story. The idea of being mistaken for dead, as is the case with Madeline Usher, had been given serious social awareness in books like Joseph Taylor's *The Danger of Premature Burial* (1819). There had been speculation about designing coffins that automatically opened should the occupant come to life; and in his story 'The Premature Burial' Poe has the narrator prepare a padded coffin to which an alarm system is attached. Poe's neurotic attraction to the idea of being coffined alive was something shared by his friend Thomas Griswold. When Griswold lost his young wife, Caroline, in 1842, he returned to her grave forty days after the funeral, had the vault unlocked, prised open the coffin, ripped off his wife's shroud and was later that evening discovered unconscious on her decomposing body.

Poe had every reason to think himself different. He attributed poetic inspiration to 'a prescient ecstasy of the beauty beyond the grave'. He saw the poet as being in dialogue with both his angels and his demons, and it was to the shadow aspects of himself that he gravitated in the writing of 'Usher'.

It is soon after the narrator's reunion with Roderick Usher that the invalid describes his symptoms. Poe is most particular in his listing of them. 'He suffered much from a morbid acuteness of the senses; the most insipid food was alone endurable; he could wear only garments of a certain texture; the odours of all flowers were oppressive; his eyes were tortured by even a faint light; and there were but peculiar sounds, and these from stringed instruments, which did not inspire him with horror.'

Usher's symptoms of acute hyperaesthesia could arguably be drawn from Poe's experiences with opium. Poe, who was the aggrandizer of an elaborate private myth aimed at a continuous distortion of self, seems to have had two alternating dependencies: opium and alcohol. Usher's behaviour may be seen as Poe's attempt to analyse his own addiction. In one of his letters Poe appears to be describing withdrawal symptoms when he writes: 'I am excessively slothful and wonderfully industrious by fits. There are epochs when any kind of mental exercise is torture . . . I have thus rambled and dreamed away whole months, and awoke, at last, to a sort of mania for composition. Then I scribble all day, and read all night, so long as the disease endures . . . I live continually in a reverie of the future.'

Roderick Usher is to embody Poe's psychological disturbances, and if his psychological traits seem to suggest the author's problems with dependency then they are accentuated by the story containing only one reference to opium. Habits are kept secret, and Usher is portrayed as no exception to an underworld lore.

Usher is, in Poe's capitalization, subject both to unspecified FEAR as well as to the peculiar obsession that his sister's death would leave him as 'the last of the ancient race of Ushers'. Opium largely kills off sexual impetus and, while the story suggests an implied incestuous relationship between brother and sister, the consummation appears psychological, for Roderick manifests all the asexual properties of a user. Roderick fears encountering absolute mental isolation, and Poe in his relationship with his tubercular wife seems to have suffered a similar fear of being left without a witness to his solitary genius.

When Poe comes to describe Madeline Usher's symptoms we see that they bear a partial resemblance to her brother's psychological disquiet. Poe records them as 'a settled apathy, a gradual wasting away of the person, and frequent though transient affections of a partially cataleptical character, were the usual diagnosis'. Brother and sister mirror each other in assuming withdrawal symptoms, only we are told that Madeline's disorder extends to catalepsy. Poe has her walk through the mansion like a somnambulist, her staring eyes seeing nothing but the internalized object of her thoughts. Poe's visual imagination is, in effect, assembling a film, and the stills have the slow-motion suspense that we have come to associate with horror movies.

Brother and sister are powerless to help each other as they belong to the same core of addiction, in the way that Poe could do little in his altered states to assist his dying wife. The opium user observes the autonomy of his unconscious images in the way that a spectator watches a film. Both are powerless to alter what they see and both are compelled to watch. It is arguable that Poe, like his creation Roderick Usher, spent a lot more time viewing his inner world than he did external events. Poe's natural resting point was distraction.

We are told that Madeline is beyond medical help and is therefore locked in with her symptoms. The narrator in the story makes no attempt to account for her disturbance but instead relies on her symptoms being reconstituted through her brother's imaginings. It is with neither subject in their right minds that Poe enters into his true *métier*, which is sensation.

The narrator, we are told, spends his days attempting to relieve

Roderick Usher's melancholy. 'We painted and read together,' he observes, 'or I listened as if in a dream, to the wild improvisations of his speaking guitar.' The narrator appears also to have entered into an altered state, for he listens 'as if in a dream' to Roderick's virtuoso guitar. And what is it here that conjures up an association with Jimi Hendrix, whose wah-wah effects seemed to speak from an atmospheric mains in a recording studio buried in the House of Usher?

Roderick improvises dirges as a commentary on his ruined state and finds release from his morbid fixations in painting. We are told that the intensity of his work is intolerable, and Poe, in describing the subject matter of one of the canvases, outlines a vision uniformly shared by opium smokers. It is of a subterranean interior lit only by the luminosity of the inner vision. Poe describes the painting as representing:

> the interior of an immensely long and rectangular vault or tunnel, with low walls, smooth, white, and without interruptions or device. Certain accessory points of the design served well to convey the idea that the excavation lay at an exceeding depth below the surface of the earth. No outlet was observed in any portion of its vast extent, and no torch, or artificial light was discernible . . .

Opium inverts appearances and it is recognizable here that the redoubtable mansion, first observed with such apprehension by the narrator, is internalized in the description of Roderick Usher's painting to represent the interiorized world of the user. This is the mental space with which Poe identifies. It is both an inviolable sanctuary which excludes the external world and a place of forbidding disquiet. This precinct may also serve as a metaphor for the self-induced atmospheric state in which the poet creates. The necessary remove from a familiar confrontation with reality is something vital to the poet at the time of writing. He needs to be both here and somewhere else. In his essay 'The Poetic Principle' Poe stated his beliefs in an inspirational drive towards spiritual vision. This visionary quest, he writes, 'belongs to the immortality of Man. It is at once a consequence and an indication of his perennial existence. It is the desire of the moth for the star. It is no mere appreciation of the Beauty before us – but a wild effort to reach the beauty above.' And, of relevance to Usher, he continues: 'Inspired by an ecstatic prescience of the glories beyond the grave, we struggle, by multiform combinations among the things and thoughts of Time, to attain a portion of that Loveliness whose very elements, perhaps, appertain to eternity alone.'

Back to Usher. That Poe was predominantly interested in mental disorder as the premises from which to create is a notion fully subscribed to by the empathetic psychological acumen he brings to his case studies of Roderick and Madeline. And we, as readers, ask the question: Is Poe writing into himself or out of himself? By that I mean is he seeking to become like his creation or is he attempting to exorcize the most destabilizing aspects of Roderick Usher from himself? Poe identified with the hero as outsider, but he was also a pathological liar whose presentation of himself in letters and in society was one of a continuous and sensationalized fiction. Poe, who was the progenitor of the thriller, also imagined himself to the be embodiment of his characters.

Roderick Usher, we are told, is subject to an acute sensitivity of the auditory nerve, which makes almost all music other than his own intolerable to his ear. He accompanies himself on guitar with lyrics written for impromptu performances. Poe describes the intensive delivery of these lyrics as comparable only to 'particular moments of the highest artificial excitement'. The narrator is the witness to a rendition of a ballad called 'The Haunted Palace'. The ballad is essentially a poem that comments on the corruption of the House of Usher and how the building's external decay is mirrored in the nerves of its subjects. In the way that the building is undermined by fungi and disrepair, so Roderick Usher's nerves have grown to be disordered through the use of opium.

Again, the idea of a guitarist with a habit of singing an off-the-wall ballad is strikingly close as a prototype to a generation of drug-damaged guitarists who have occupied public consciousness via rock music in the second half of the twentieth century.

Roderick Usher describes to the narrator how he imagines himself to have become the house. An architecture has, through psychic osmosis, become a neurology. But the manner in which Poe has Usher account for this sense of bizarre metamorphosis is through an obsession with the house's structural collapse. Poe tells us that Usher is unnaturally preoccupied with 'the method of collocation of these stones – in order of their arrangement, as well as in that of the many fungi which over-spread them, and of the decayed trees which stood around – above all, in the long undisturbed endurance of this arrangement, and in its reduplication in the still waters of the tarn'.

In psychological terms Poe has Roderick Usher anticipate breakdown. Roderick is poised on the edge of mental collapse. He stares at his encroaching madness aware that only escape into opium can afford him respite from the impending crash. The house will come down simultaneously with his sanity.

Poe had plenty of time in his short life to witness in his wife, Virginia, the stages of protracted tuberculosis referred to as 'death-in-life'. Virginia's periods of haemorrhaging from her lungs and consequent bleeding from her mouth proved the sort of agonizing slow crawl to death-states that feature in Poe's stories. Poe heightened his mystique by living cut off from the world with a wife who was in fact a cousin and a protective aunt. It can be assumed that Usher's compulsive phobia concerning his sister's health is a metaphor for the anxiety that Poe suffered in watching his young wife's gradual death. In his essay 'The Philosophy of Consumption' Poe had written: 'The death, then, of a beautiful woman is, unquestionably, the most poetic topic in the world . . .' It is not impossible that Poe married his valetudinarian cousin in order to exalt her when dead.

It is with imperturbable cool that Poe has Roderick announce to the narrator on the death of his sister that his intention is to preserve her corpse for two weeks prior to burial in one of the mansion's underground vaults. From this point onwards in the story Madeline enters into the most favoured of Poe's psychological categories – the undead. Poe's largely unfocused sexual energies seem to have fired only in response to some extraterrestrial sexual union.

It is in the description of the two men, Roderick and the narrator, carrying Madeline in an open coffin to rest in a vault located at a great depth beneath the house that Poe's visual imagination anticipates film. The sombre, perfectly motioned prose is directed like a sequence of film stills, as the two men carrying their burden descend through oppressive levels to a vault that had once been used as a dungeon. Like the interior of Roderick's painting this cell, which serves as a vault, also admits no light. The two men in their journey to the centre of the underworld may also be seen to be carrying a perverse Pandora's box. The contents of Pandora's box should never be observed, but the two men are compelled to lift the coffin lid and look inside. The narrator's discovery comprises the realization that brother and sister have an uncommon facial resemblance. Madeline, who is described as cataleptic, is observed by the narrator as retaining colour and as having a smile on her lips. Poe can be observed infecting the narrative charge with the idea of a vampire, and it is within the precinct of the vampirical that Poe's libido finds itself alert.

If we continue with the notion of Poe directing his film then the visuals are sustained throughout the sequential paragraph in which the two men return to the house. The shift in atmosphere is accompanied by a shift in Roderick Usher's behaviour and the alteration of his symptoms are attributed by Poe to the advent of madness. The madness that Poe describes, a condition characterized by the subject's apathy and derealization, suggests the severe withdrawal symptoms of a junkie.

We are advised that Roderick sits in a vacant attitude for hours on end, staring at nothing and appearing to listen to some imaginary sound. Poe implies that Roderick is internalized to a degree that makes no allowance for the external world. The addict exchanges time for space. Wherever the cursor points, it's to inner configurations and the endless preoccupying stream of imagery that comments on psyche.

Poe, who was presumed never to have smiled, lived in a state of ravaging and humiliating poverty, often driven to eat nothing but bread and molasses for days on end. His letters chew the paper with their urgent commentary on his indigence. His occasional forays into literary society, or attempts made to join the lecturing circuit, invariably ended in disgrace and drunkenness. Opium would have offered him a private space in which to amplify his feelings of dissociation from humanity. Poe's fantasy would have been to have lived like the Ushers in a Gothic mansion at a remove from the world. And Poe would ideally, like Roderick Usher, have lived in possession of an inherited wealth that would have allowed him to pursue his solitary occupations.

Speculation A: It is Roderick who is a woman and Madeline who is a man.

Speculation B: Both have desexualized themselves in terms of gender after consummating incest.

Speculation C: Pseudo-necrophilic sex takes place in the coffin.

It is with great narrative skill that Poe succeeds in bringing his subject to the edge of fragmentation. Roderick, who appears to the narrator to be in possession of an unrepeatable secret, has not adjusted after his journey to the underworld. His return has involved no release from his symptoms. His consciousness is over-visual and he has not obeyed the dictates of the sacrificial mysteries, which involve averting the eyes from the dead. In this sense, both Usher and the narrator have violated the mystery surrounding Madeline's death. They have, in their going inward, desacralized the object of their journey and return in the way of Orpheus who similarly dishonours Eurydice.

Through the ritual of a journey to the interior Poe creates an aftermath of suspense that prepares the reader for Madeline's destructive return. Madeline is to return as a recriminative Fury whose vampirical desire for revenge results in the annihilation of the House of Usher.

The narrator and Roderick have emerged as criminals from the contained space that characterizes the underworld. There's a distinct possibility that they have sexually violated Madeline, something implied by Poe's sensual aggrandizement of her corpse. But important here is the commitment to irrevocable experience. The journey had to be made, in the way that events happen in life without our asking for them, and both men embody their experience as witnesses to something profound without searching to correct what has happened. They resurface as the experience of their encounter. They now have no choice but to live out the nemetic consequences of their actions.

In a letter to a friend, written in 1845, Poe had stressed: 'I find myself entirely myself – dreadfully sick and depressed but still myself. I seem to have just awakened from some horrible dream, in which all was confusion . . . I really believe that I have been mad.'

The author's predicament is transferred to Usher. The journey to the underworld has permitted Roderick the chance to re-vision his obsessions. If he has believed that he would one day be free of his habit, as Poe must have sometimes convinced himself, then he is in danger of exchanging an artificial reality for a worse state of consciousness. The dream topos speaks through images. We detach from its visuals by opening our eyes. Poe as a matter of terror has Usher duplicate inner and outer realities. The building or skull in which he lives is internalized in his opium reveries and externalized in the hours in which he chooses to make contact with the outside. We are told throughout the story that Usher spends his time watching but we never learn what he sees. Instead, he is listening, or he is attempting to see what he hears. This confusion of the senses is used by Poe to convey the opium experience. What the story narrates is an extension of Roderick's vacancy. He is outwardly indisposed to relate the contents of what he sees as a user.

Having finally located Usher in madness, and more than that an awareness of the constituents of his difference, Poe prepares the reader for the inner and outer storm that is finally to break over the House of Usher. Though Poe may be seen to borrow heavily from the Gothic tradition of an isolated castle attracting a storm, he differs from the genre in his psychological portrayal of madness as central to the elemental denouement.

In his essay 'The Philosophy of Composition' Poe had affirmed that 'Beauty is the sole legitimate province of the poem', and he ascribed this notion to a quality of soul, rather than to heart or intellect. Roderick's illness is located in psyche, or soul, and while he remains vitally alive to the aesthetic properties of beauty he inverts the register so that he is confronted by the shadow, or the underside, of his attraction. He also lives in the shadow side of sexuality, which is incest and a necrophilic attraction to the body.

In his essay on composition Poe linked the concept of beauty to melancholy. He wrote: 'Beauty of whatever kind, in its supreme development, invariably excites the sensitive soul to tears. Melancholy is thus the most legitimate of all poetical tones.'

Roderick Usher might be described as the personification of melancholy, in the way that Poe was similarly observed to be disconsolate by his contemporaries.

If Poe was speaking in his essay of those smoky, lowlight moods that have us gravitate to poetry, then the climactic pages of 'Usher' are informed by a shift from melancholy to implosive apocalypse.

It is a week after Madeline's burial in a subterranean vault that the narrator, on retiring to bed, experiences a state of extreme panic. The sunken furniture in his room and the intimations of a rising storm are the special effects or soundtrack that Poe employs to heighten the Gothic aspects of his story. What Poe is really describing is the unspecified anxiety associated with withdrawal. He calls it 'an incubus of utterly causeless alarm'. And because Poe is describing his own state of psychological discomfort, he comes to impart Usher's symptoms to the narrator, so that both men follow a simultaneous arc of hysteria.

When Usher, similarly alerted to incipient feelings of terror, arrives at the narrator's room, Poe reports on 'a species of mad hilarity in his eyes – an evidently restrained hysteria in his whole demeanour'. Poe describes his subject in the way that his young wife and companion aunt must so often have observed him. Poe is seeing himself.

The external cause of Usher's demented state is that of a whirlwind which seems to have localized itself around the house. But underpinning the wind's unpredictable velocity is a luminous aura that invests the house, the decaying trees and the black tarn. Given that Roderick Usher is photophobic, the unnatural intensity of light entering his visual field triggers severe crisis. And with the perverse sense of lighting one fire with another, Poe turns up the volume of his story by having the narrator read the 'Mad Trist of Sir Launcelot Canning' to the agitated Roderick Usher.

Poe opportunely relates a story within a story and concentrates on the part of the Mad Trist in which Ethelred, the hero of the tale, having been denied entry to the hermit's dwelling forces his way into the place by ripping down the door. Using the subtext for analogy, Poe has Usher and the narrator correspondingly grow aware of the sound of wood being torn apart in the mansion's depths. Usher has clearly come into the narrator's space as he is pacted to the latter's involvement as a witness or participant in the violation of the dead. The narrator has been a co-presence to Usher's pathological improprieties. But what looks like a possible death pact is not to be. The singular current of malevolent tension shared between brother and sister is non-transferable. Roderick Usher's individual destiny is inexorably linked to his sister's, and the tragedy investing their bonded death wish is one that excludes the story's narrator. They differ in the one being fixed and the other primed for flight.

The metaphor in which the subtext invests is extended by Poe to take in the passage of how Ethelred, on breaking into the hermit's hut, discovers no sign of the holy man but in his place a dragon situated before a gold palace. The dragon sits in front of a shield on which is written: 'Who entereth herein, a conqueror hath bin; Who slayeth the dragon, the shield he shall win.'

Ethelred dispatches the dragon, and the beast's shrieking death agonies are taken up within the main story by the narrator's awareness of a scream issuing from within the house. We notice again Poe's distinct mirroring of inner with outer as well as the place of aural imagination within the arena of disturbance. Both the narrator and Usher are dependent on imagining the dragon's scream, for it takes place within a story. Madeline's scream is also silent to the reader and it's the imagination that imparts sound to the work. How, we may ask, did Poe hear the double scream within his narrative? It may have originated in an opium trance and evolved from one of those windowless white spaces that Poe visited when under the drug's influence. It is clear from most of Poe's stories that he orchestrated his sound effects from a core of repressed hysteria. Poe, who was known for his silence, has most of his characters scream.

Roderick Usher is described as orientated towards the source of disturbance. Poe has him position his chair so that he sits facing the door. The question of escape is never considered as an option: Usher remains paralysed. There is nowhere to hide because the terror is both within and without. When another passage in the subtext prepares us for the vengeance that has always been coming, Poe has Usher rise and give voice to his extreme fear. He claims to have been aware of his sister's movements in the coffin for days. He has all the time been able to hear her heart beating, he says, through the stone walls and floors of the house.

Usher's exclamation, 'We have put her living in the tomb', reads like a partial attempt on his part to implicate the narrator in sexual guilt. Twice Usher shrieks out the word 'MADMAN', as though passing judgement on himself, the narrator and their actions.

Madeline's revenge is final and hysterical. When the door is blown open by the wind, the two men see her standing outside in a bloodstained shroud. What ensues is like a blood wedding, a demonic reunion in which brother and sister die in convulsive combat. In keeping with the sensations of imagined suffocation that withdrawal induces, Poe has Madeline fall on top of her brother, as an unbearable weight on his diaphragm. The shock of the encounter kills Roderick outright and he dies, according to Poe, as 'a victim to the terrors he anticipated'.

Madeline was placed on her back in the coffin, and in the vampirical rites that constitute the killing of her brother her position is reversed: she dies face forward, as though the polarities of gender have been changed and it is Roderick who is the woman and Madeline who is the dominant male.

The narrator has, of necessity, to escape the death pact shared by the brother and sister in order to narrate the contents of the story. In his flight he is aware of a scarlet moon shining direct through the zigzag fissures in the house. It is this red planet, which could arguably be construed as a metaphor for alien intelligence, which activates the house being instantly torched. The narrator is a witness to apocalypse. He sees the house swallowed by the waters in which previously he had studied its reflection. There is no remission. Everything disappears. Roderick and his sister, locked in their final embrace, return to the deep waters of the unconscious.

I am not proposing that Poe gained any psychological release from writing this story, but he probably reflected on it for a day or two after its completion. 'If in many of my productions terror has been the thesis,' he wrote, 'I maintain that terror is not of Germany, but of the soul, that I have deduced this terror only from its legitimate sources, and urged it only to its legitimate results.' Refuting critical charges that his stories were infected with German romanticism, Poe speaks truthfully of the arena in which he discovered his subject matter. Images live in psyche, and the House of Usher is a building constructed from imagery. Poe was only at one with himself in that interior.

At the time of writing 'Usher' Poe stood at five feet eight inches tall, slim, with black curly hair, grey eyes, disproportionately broad forehead, his customary quiet being emphasized by a dejected manner. He would not have been missed in a crowd, and he liked that. He had the death-in-life oscillation of his wife's health with which to contend. There was journalism. The bottle. Opium. Money problems. There wasn't much time to reflect on his achievements of the imagination. The perverse in him would have said that he wrote with the intention of shocking his contemporaries. I would say that he wrote with the intention of shocking his contemporaries into an awareness of imagination. That was his place. And it is to this house that the narrator of Poe's story comes in order to be initiated in a journey to the underworld. What he discovered was a loop. The way in was the way out, only everything changed in the process of getting there. Poe probably had a drink on finishing his narrative, had a second and a third one for consolation and went out to post his story – not to a magazine but to posterity.

SAINT OSCAR

SAINT Oscar. I want to reflect on according Wilde the epithet of sainthood, in the same way that Jean-Paul Sartre saw fit to entitle his prodigiously analytic study of Jean Genet *Saint Genet, comédien et martyr*. Both Wilde and Genet were to suffer prolonged prison sentences and humanly and imaginatively to transcend the appalling indignities and depradation that were coexistent with loss of liberty. If it is easy to see in both men an archetypal affinity with the figure of Saint Sebastian, his agonized body bleeding with arrows, then the analogy is perhaps made good only by a society seeking, in time, to redress and modify the penal strictures by which it outlaws those who dare to be different.

Saint Oscar. Society favourite and reviled exile. Aesthete and criminal. Do you know what colour eyes he had? It's important to know that they were blue if you are truly to empathize with his suffering. Wilde has in a way been the victim of too notorious a posthumous legacy. His work and his life are out of balance and, as biographically stimulating as the life may be, the work also carries a subversive and altogether durable bite. Do you know his body-weight and whether he dyed his eyelashes or how he spread his hands? You need to think of these things, not only to reanatomize and recharacterize Wilde but also to unite the physiological organism with the work. The thrust, the counterdrive, the dynamic behind creativity, are generated by particular psychic and physical impulses. An individuated neurology.

In *The Picture of Dorian Gray*, the novel in which Wilde made public his beliefs about homosexuality and a work which was used by the prosecution as saliently distorted evidence with which to convict him, Wilde gave voice to the vision of a new city and a corresponding felicity for its inhabitants. It's a side of Wilde which has been neglected, the poet searching for an external counterpart to his inner vision. Wilde lived by night and for its nocturnal excesses; he feared intrusive recrimination for his love of 'feasting with panthers'. Like all those who live by the senses, he grew tired of having endlessly to repeat the need for heightened sensation and looked towards the arrival of the new day, one in which need would be assuaged and the threat of the past eliminated. Wilde anticipates a time when:

> our eyelids might open some morning upon a world that had been refashioned anew in the darkness for our pleasure, a world in which things would have fresh shapes and colours, and be changed, or have other secrets, a world in which the past would have little or no place, or survive, at any rate, in no conscious form of obligation or regret, the remembrance even of joy having its bitterness, and the memories of pleasure their pain.

While it's possible to view these sentiments as congruent with Wilde's insatiably hedonistic pursuits, there is here a reaching towards the visionary city, the metaphorical architectonics of which are built into the aspirations of the imaginative poets. London was Wilde's nearest reference point, his West End nucleus taking in Kettner's in Greek Street, the Café Royal in Regent's Street, Brown's Hotel, Claridge's – and wasn't it his visionary hope that his city would be transformed according to poetic anticipation? The imagination becoming reality, in the way that Wilde's own fear of age is transferred to Dorian Gray's endless deferral of that issue in *The Picture of Dorian Gray*. The bitter-sweet twist in Wilde's life was that his aspirations to achieve permanent youth could be granted him only through the imaginative reality of his writing. But all writing is a travelling away from the self, a journey of departure endlessly heading to the right-hand side of the page. The poet gains and loses in the same action; the celebratory impulse in Wilde turns on the edge of elegy, as the poet is confronted with the realization that his vision is denied reality off the page.

Saint Oscar. Beneath the provocative 'I represent to you all the sins you have never had the courage to commit', 'I' was the idealist attempting to find in aestheticism the sort of transcendent ideal that would revision the universe. Wilde was subversively impatient with the moral straitjacketing imposed by the regulations of Victorian fiction, and *The Picture of Dorian Gray* can be seen as the beginnings of a British counterculture, a novel that would prove seminal to underground writing in the twentieth century: 'I consider that for any man of culture to accept the standard of his age, is a form of the grossest immorality,' he writes. And in *The Soul of Man Under Socialism* he repeats his conviction: 'Any attempt to extend the subject matter of art is extremely distasteful to the public; and yet the vitality and progress of art depend in a large measure on the continual extension of the subject-matter.' Wilde's novel, while it draws heavily on the influence of Huysmans' *A Rebours*, that quintessential compendium of decadent pursuits, is none the less original and shocking, a necessary marriage of virtues to an idealist attempting to expand frontiers of tolerance.

I see *The Picture of Dorian Gray* as a novel concerned with nocturnal apocalypse and with altered states of consciousness, as well as being the psychological narrative of an author intent on risking self-abasement in the pursuit of truth. Wilde as sinner and saint but always in the interest of the imagination. Proust chose to work at night as a conspiratorial pact with inner silence, and some of the most illuminating actions in Wilde's novel belong to the great book of the night written in by angels. Wilde needed to steep himself in the shadow-side of life in order to enhance spiritual awareness. What was he looking for? Most probably spiritual gold. Wilde is his own most eloquent commentator on the subject:

> People thought it dreadful of me to have entertained at dinner the evil things of life, and to have found pleasure in their company. But they, from the point of view through which I, as an artist in life, approached them, were delightfully suggestive and stimulating. It was like feasting with panthers. The danger was half the excitement. I used to feel as the snake charmer must when he lures the cobra to stir from the painted cloth or reed-basket that holds it, and makes it spread its hood at his bidding, and sway to and fro in the air as a plant sways restfully in a stream.

The danger for Wilde was the excitement, and a corresponding stimulus informs the best passages of *The Picture of Dorian Gray*. Experience itself is without moral attachment and achieves that status only through retrospective evaluation. Wilde had developed a schema for living in which sexual experience couldn't be separated from his visionary nocturnal quest. Wilde's panthers were correspondingly black angels volatilized with poetry. They were intermediaries whose possible redemption pointed towards the new day. Wilde's pick-up places, like the Alhambra, the Pavilion, the Empire and the bar at St James's, and his destination after that, the private room at Kettner's, were stations of the cross towards his eventual martyrdom. Poetic conception occupied him in the journey. Attracted to his opposites, he sensitized the underworld in his psyche and grew fascinated by his capacities to live a dual existence. There's a night passage in *Dorian Gray* in which Wilde reflects on Dorian's dichotomized life, which reads as a template of autobiography:

> There were moments, indeed, at night, when, lying sleepless in his own delicately-scented chamber, or in the sordid room of the little ill-famed tavern near the Docks, which, under an assumed name, and in disguise, it was his habit to frequent, he would think of the ruin he had brought upon his soul, with a pity that was all the more poignant because it was purely selfish. But moments such as these were rare . . . The more he knew, the more he desired to know. He had mad hungers that grew more ravenous as he fed them.

Wilde's poetic vision, one of Dionysian exploration, is the very opposite of the defeatist plasmitoxosis which has invaded so much mid- to late-twentieth-century British poetry, with its reductionist negativity working as a countervailing force to imaginative vision. His work is about expansion and the apprehension of the transcendental as it is sighted through poetry. Wilde attempted to have life blaze on his pulses. The effects would be like biting into a strawberry spiked with hallucinogens. His credo to instate a new poetry and a vital awareness of the immediate 'was to be experience itself, and not the fruits of experience, sweet or bitter as they might be. Of the asceticism that deadens the senses, as of the vulgar profligacy that dulls them, it was to know nothing. But it was to teach man to concentrate upon the moments of a life that is itself but a moment.'

Experience itself as the criterion for poetry is a rare phenomenon, and part of the genuine human risk to which Wilde subjected himself was motivated by the experiential need to find life in poetry and poetry in life. He went out in search of fallen angels in the London streets. The night is a time of waiting in expectation for some remedial transformation to show at break of day. There is a history of night writing. It permeates Shakespeare's brooding tragedies, it is the subject of Edward Young's *Night Thoughts*, Novalis' *Hymns to the Night*, Rimbaud's *A Season in Hell*, Rilke's angelically permeated *Duino Elegies*, and it is the Dionysiac provenance informing writers as diverse as Beckett, Genet, Céline and Burroughs. Cities change at night. Who knows if, when crossing Waterloo Bridge in the early hours, we won't encounter the leader of a new species, a walk-in carrying a revelatory message as to how to unlock consciousness and immortality as it is coded in our DNA? Having the keys to the city means symbolically learning the secrets of death. Wilde in his own way subscribed to Blake's proverb: 'The road of excess leads to the palace of wisdom.' There could be no turning back on that road, and Wilde followed it right to the end.

Wilde reflected long on the night. There's a chemical optimism, a crowding of endorphins released by the brain, which may create the unnatural excitement we experience in the hours when we should be sleeping. He knew, too, the disquiet which often comes at the hour before dawn, when the mind considers its unresolved chimeras and sleeplessness is tuned to the reproachful volume of a disquieted conscience. Wilde, who increasingly came to be subjected to blackmail and to buying back the imprudent letters he had sent to 'panthers', remarks in *Dorian Gray* on waking at dawn to discover 'the half-cut book that we had been studying, or the wired flower that we had worn at the ball, or the letter that we had been afraid to read, or that we had read too often'. But there were times on returning to Tite Street, or the hotel at which he was staying, when the night must have appeared apocalyptic to Wilde. Anything and everything was possible, and the gold key to the night was safe in his pocket. What do we know of tomorrow when we would extend the night to its optimum potential?

The Picture of Dorian Gray reads prophetically of its author's own fall from grace both prior to and subsequent to his imprisonment in 1895. We are a hundred years on, but pain and humiliation still smell and feel and taste the same. In the novel he evokes the scandal surrounding his name, and the ostracism he was to suffer, through Dorian's periodic immersion in low life. Wilde writes:

> It was rumoured that he had been seen brawling with foreign sailors in a low den in the distant parts of Whitechapel, and that he consorted with thieves and coiners, and knew the mysteries of their trade. His extraordinary absences became notorious, and, when he used to reappear again in society, men would whisper to each other in corners, or pass him with a sneer, or look at him with cold searching eyes, as though they were determined to discover his secrets.

What does it mean to be different? The clue to Wilde's secret wasn't just in his sexuality; it lay more in his refusal to accept aspects of life made conditional by ideological protocol. Gender conformity, capitalist employment within a corrupt system, the credo of the romantic poet has always been to rebel against individual restraint. Today poets have joined the system and seceded the dignity that comes with the role of being a poet, and implicit in that calling is the non-separation of the life from the work. And isn't this where Wilde differed? He refused to concede to the principle of secure employment and chose instead to risk siding with the unconventional. Poets who have the temerity to be undeviatingly true to their vision are rarely favoured by a literary establishment. Wilde, whose liberating vision looked towards aesthetic and sexual ameliorations in a closed ethos, beliefs which necessarily implied conflict with society, gravitated towards a nocturnal milieu who also lived on the edge of society. 'Panthers' were using another means of getting back at society, and it was catastrophic that Wilde should eventually prove the effigial victim of an underground he was seeking to endorse through the writing of his novel. In other words, Wilde's literary deviance demanded a corresponding physical fulfilment. His defiant dress, his irreverent maxims, the wit with which he undermined social strictures, the ostentation and generosity he brought to any company and the success he achieved as a playwright during the early years of the 1890s, were all facets of his brilliant afflatus which were to attract the attention of confirmed enemies. Wilde also differed from his contemporaries in that he externalized his inner life through his clothes. Turning up at the offices of William Heinemann on his thirty-seventh birthday, Wilde was dressed in a black morning suit. Offered condolences over what was assumed to be a bereavement, Wilde explained: 'This day happens to be my birthday, and I am mourning, as I shall henceforth do on each of my anniversaries, the flight of one year of my youth into nothingness, the growing blight upon my summer.' And it's exactly this form of romanticized audacity that we celebrate in Wilde's extraordinary capacity to live in the moment and savour it like biting into the sharply sweet apprehension of a cherry. And if we knew nothing about Wilde but that single action we would consider him extraordinary.

In 1891, a year after the publication of *The Picture of Dorian Gray*, we get a physical impression of Wilde, at the time of a visit to Paris, by the French writer Marcel Schwob. Schwob described Wilde as:

> A big man with a large pasty face, red cheeks, an ironic eye, bad and protrusive teeth, a vicious childlike mouth with soft lips . . . While he ate – and he ate little – he never stopped smoking opium-tainted Egyptian cigarettes. A terrible absinthe-drinker, through which he got his visions and desires.

Wilde was in fact six feet in height, and imposing. I mention this in respect of his visibility in the night. He couldn't make less of himself and was not to be forgotten by those he encountered. Height six feet and body-weight around fourteen and a half stone. Wilde's particular genius demanded a public day and night. Every act of his was, in a way, a performance, and it was his natural inability to conceal all aspects of his exuberant life expression that was to lead to his social ruin. Wilde's belief in the absolute authority of the poet, the artist privileged to encounter all experience without moral prohibition, was, to say the least, dangerously controversial:

> When Benvenuto Cellini crucified a living man to study the play of muscles in his death agony, a pope was right to grant him absolution. What is the death of a vague individual if it enables an immortal word to blossom and to create, in Keats' words, an eternal source of ecstasy?

Views like these, and the inviolable sanctity Wilde afforded the artist, were likely to provide ridicule and hostility from those unwilling to commit themselves to his singular programme. Part of Wilde's nocturnal daring came about through his conviction that the artist should be free to experience every form of individual fulfilment. Wilde's West End of London represented to him a mythic underworld presided over by Hermaphroditus, with a retinue of panthers in attendance. That was 1895. If we then jump a century's a quantum leap to 1995 when I wrote this poem, 'West End Dilemma':

The roar's like thunder in a bottleneck.
Placement, displacement in the pouring crowd,
I straighten out in St Anne's Court,
a respite from the crazed genome
and read in the scrambled graffiti text
our writing's on the wall.
A bold disjointed voodoo hex.
And sometimes in the Soho streets
I anticipate meeting William Blake
leading two lions on a leash
down Wardour Street. The sunlight's over-reach
gets violently through traffic haze.
A rent-boy paints a fingernail
inside a cappuccino bar.
We're now and always in the little time
permitted us in which to live,
a bite at the immediate. I hear
my blood like a waterfall in my head,
my haemoglobins, DNA.
It's afternoon, the time I go in search

of what I never find. I stay a while
in this tight alley between streets,
prepare myself, then go back to the wild
insistent pressure building to the sun.

But if Wilde lived by night in the expansion of psychosexual energies we shouldn't forget the aesthetic refinement of his attachment to daytime observations and his unashamed celebration of beauty in whatever form he discovered it. Few novels open with such an immediate, hedonistic tang of perfume and light as *The Picture of Dorian Gray*: 'The studio was filled with the rich odour of roses, and when the light summer wind stirred amidst the trees of the garden there came through the open door the heavy scent of the lilac, or the more delicate perfume of the pink-flowering thorn –' This olfactory cocktail has associations in common with Proust, another writer who was to conjugate memory with scent. The love of flowers was never to leave Wilde and, his health irreparably broken by the punitive measures he experienced in prison, he was to associate the idea of freedom with the anticipation of spring flowers evident in London. 'I tremble with pleasure,' he wrote, 'when I think that on the very day of my leaving prison both the laburnum and the lilac will be blooming in the gardens, and that I shall see the wind stir into restless beauty the swaying gold of the one, and make the other toss the pale purple of its plumes so that all the air shall be Arabia for me.' How, I wonder, was Sir Alfred Wills, the prosaic judge who had passed sentence on Wilde, viewing his spring? I imagine the beauties of laburnum and lilac would have left him cold.

Wilde was a lifelong appreciator of perfumes and, in writing to Hore Adey in anticipation of his release from Reading, he listed among his wants:

Some nice French soap, Houbigant's if you can get it, either 'Peau d'Espagne' or 'Sac de Laitue' . . . Also, some scent; Canterbury Wood Violet I would like, and some 'Eau du Lubin' for the toilet, a large bottle . . . My hair has become very grey: I am under the impression that it's quite white, but I believe that is an exaggeration: there is a wonderful thing called Koko Marikopas, to be got at 233 Regent Street, which is a wonderful hair-tonic: the name alone seems worth the money, so please get a large bottle.

These items of Oscariana are not ephemeral, they are complementary to his spiritual needs, the accoutrements which contributed to his fine tuning. Wilde understandably felt the need to purge himself of prison life and to be cleansed of the whole contaminating patina of his cell.

If I was asked to define hell I would, without reservation, call it the spirit of institutions: those who think in terms of a collective and constraining mediocrity; those who deny individual advance and difference. Poetry is a vital antidote to an institutionalized rationale. It's a vital shot of adrenalin into a dead organism. Its truth is a means of redressing lies propagated by the media. Wilde antagonized the enemy, was too verbally dextrous for his detractors and had the effrontery to live out his triumphant contentions in public. What the judiciary attempted to put in a cage was not only the accused but also the imagination. Wilde's triumphant revenge was, of course, in the writing of 'The Ballad of Reading Gaol', a poem which was to afford him a posterity unlikely to be achieved by members of the judiciary.

Saint Oscar. But the humiliation was insufferable. In words underscored with blood he recounted his acute tribulations in 'De Profundis', not the least of which was being exposed to vehement public ridicule at Clapham Junction. Wilde writes:

> From two o'clock till half-past two on that day I had to stand on the centre platform of Clapham Junction in convict dress and handcuffed, for all the world to look at . . . Of all possible objects I was the most grotesque. When people saw me they laughed. Each train as it came up swelled the audience. Nothing could exceed their amusement. That was of course before they knew who I was. As soon as they had been informed, they laughed still more. For half an hour I stood there in the grey November rain surrounded by a jeering mob. For a year after that was done to me I wept every day at the same hour and for the same space of time.

He omits to report here that hecklers were also permitted to spit in his face.

Though Wilde was physically and mentally destroyed by prison, his imagination transcended it. And did that imagination sit like a ball of gold light opposite him in his cell? Was he comforted by its angelicized potential, in the way that Rilke, in a period of creative aridity, went out on to the roof at Duino and heard a voice in the wind enunciate the first lines of his hard-won *Duino Elegies*. For two years Wilde conducted a solitary dialogue with the imagination, that most protean, metamorphic and marvellous of phenomena, a faculty which not only kept him sane but one that proved untouchable by the authorities. Trying to kill the imagination is like a cat watching a fish behind an aquarium glass.

There is a discomforting inevitability about Wilde's self-destructive nocturnal habits in the years leading up to 1895 which suggest that his destiny was precisely the one he needed to follow. Fascinated by a nightlife which he knew would explode in his face, Wilde was pushed by a wind at his back to follow experience to the interior. He sleepwalked his way into the opposing traffic:

For beauty's nothing
but the beginning of terror, we're hardly able to bear
and we're fascinated because it serenely disdains
to destroy us. Every angel's terrible.

These are Rilke's lines from the first of the *Duino Elegies* and they have a particular pertinence to Wilde. He, too, must have come to consider every angel terrifying. And at the end they turned against him. Black smoking arrows were picked from their bodies and placed in his heart. And these angels had human names: Edward Shelley, Sidney Mavor, Maurice Schwabe, Alfred Wood, Charles Parker, Walter Grainger, Alfonso Conway. Conceiving of these characters as alumni attracted to his genius, mythic components in his nocturnal journey, Wilde must have been horrified to encounter them as recriminative opponents in a court. They were all given exemption from prosecution and paid by Lord Alfred Douglas's father, the Marquess of Queensbury, to testify against Wilde. Wilde's trial was one in which the demystification of his past was as savage as the sentence given him.

My proposition is that Wilde's genius, which risked a flippancy, a dazzling surface exterior in the plays, required a correcting immersion in the nightside of life, and his great works, *The Picture of Dorian Gray*, 'De Profundis' and 'The Ballad of Reading Gaol', are all symptomatic of a willingness voluntarily to explore the shadow. In reflection, Wilde wrote:

I let myself be lured into long spells of senseless and sensual ease. I amused myself with being a *flâneur*, a dandy, a man of fashion. I surrounded myself with the smaller natures and the meaner minds . . . Tired of being on the heights, I deliberately went to the depths in the

search for new sensations. What the paradox was to me in the sphere of
thought, perversity became to me in the sphere of passion.

Arthur Rimbaud, the intransigently defiant visionary genius
of modern poetry, had, while still a schoolboy, propounded a credo
for the poet which involved the systematic derangement of the
senses and the directive to renounce all personal safety in aspiring
to know imaginative truth through hallucinated perception.
Rimbaud's insistence on the poet using his mind and body as the
sounding-board for expansive experiential perception demanded
a courage that few were prepared to follow. Rimbaud's almost
shamanistic apprehension of poetry as delirium, or as a controlled
reversible psychosis in which the poet discovered new colours,
new sounds, new universes, was, to a certain degree, knowingly
lived out in Wilde's exploration of the night. Rimbaud encountered extreme poverty, vagrancy and social rejection in his brief
years as a poet, restlessly moving from city to city and country to
country in pursuit of his poetic ideal. Rimbaud, who was to aban-
don the writing of poetry before he was twenty, turned away from
his dynamic with feelings of bitter disillusionment and disappointment. He said goodbye to the world in his profoundly
illuminating prose poem, *A Season in Hell*, and became an arms
dealer in the Sahara, exchanging one anti-social medium for
another.

Wilde's search for what he called 'new sensations' involved the
eventual ordeal of prison, but *The Picture of Dorian Gray* was the
triumphant expression of his imaginative journey to the end of the
night. With characteristic courage Wilde succeeded in his novel to
make manifest 'the other side of life'. Unwilling any longer to separate his instincts from his art, Wilde gave free expression to his
psychosexual vision in a fiction which exonerates beauty at the

expense of its detractors and celebrates individual growth at the cost of those who would settle for collective spiritual inertia. The system was impotent to break him. Writing from prison he found renewed strength in the concept of the individual:

> People used to say of me that I was too individualistic. I must be far more of an individualist than I ever was. I must get far more out of myself than I ever got, and ask for less of the world than ever I asked. Indeed, my ruin came not from too great indivi-dualism of life, but from too little. The one disgraceful, unpardonable, and to all time contemptible action of my life was to allow myself to appeal to Society for help and protec-tion. To have made such an appeal would have been from the individualist's point of view bad enough, but what excuse can there ever be put forward for having made it?

It takes genius to find unequivocal strength in self-conviction in the way that Wilde expresses it here. Wilde had lost everything but himself. Redemption is an inner process, and Wilde worked on it with selfless devotion. The existential crisis in his life came too late to form the matrix of a new artistic expression, but Wilde inside prison developed limitless reserves of compassion for the suffering and a philosophic understanding of the nature of experi-ence which looked more to the poetics of Blake, Rimbaud and Nietzsche than to the aesthetics of Walter Pater which Wilde had earlier on adopted as his poetic criterion. Writing from prison, and evaluating an inhuman ordeal for which nothing in his life could have prepared him, Wilde spoke of the unremittingly circu-lar nature of his suffering:

> Suffering is one long moment. We cannot divide it by seasons. We can only record its moods, and chronicle their returns. With us time itself

does not progress. It revolves. It seems to circle round one centre of pain. The paralysing immobility of a life every circumstance of which is regulated after an unchangeable pattern, so that we eat and drink and lie down or pray, or at least kneel for prayer, according to the inflexible laws of an iron formula: this immobile quality, that makes each dreadful day in the very minutest detail like its brother, seems to communicate itself to those external forces, the very essence of whose existence is ceaseless change.

Wilde was detained in a cell thirteen by seven by nine feet, with a single opaque glass window above the floor. And it took seven months before he was allowed any supply of prison paper on which to write. He pleaded the threat of mental breakdown and the debilitation of his literary gifts, but prison doctors considered his mind too lucid to be under any threat of insanity.

Wilde is writing here from experience that he shouldn't have had to assimilate in this manner but none the less converted into the imaginative province of his last two works, 'De Profundis' and 'The Ballad of Reading Gaol'. He should have arrived at this knowledge in the way, for instance, that Shakespeare wins his psychological territory from profound empathy with every form of extreme behavioural aberration: murder, incest, patricide, matricide, martial and tyrannical atrocity.

I want to return to the theme of the night. Some of the most evocatively atmospheric passages in *The Picture of Dorian Gray* are the ones in which Dorian visits the Limehouse opium dens. Wilde's writing flattens itself on the page with the alert stealth of a cat. Attracted again to his opposite, this time in terms of a physical and sociological environment, Wilde portrays Dorian's desperate search for kicks in opium houses by the docks with the authenticity of someone who either participated in those nocturnal excursions or mixed with people who could describe such places to him. The narrated thrust of Dorian's night journeys across the city, with fog making the going perilous and marauding thieves likely to attack the driver, resonate with a facility for risk which was absent from Wilde's British contemporaries. 'To cure the soul by means of the senses and the senses by means of the soul' was the nocturnal paradox on which Wilde deliberated, choosing action as the best means of discourse. His evocative prose gets the East End docks into focus with all the qualities of a photographer's infra-red slow exposure. Dorian's conspiratorial pact with opium finds its external qualification in the presence of docks, the river's swollen eye, the brooding hulks of ships:

> Here and there a lantern gleamed at the stern of some huge merchant-man. The light shook and splintered in the puddles. A red glare came from an outward-bound steamer that was coaling. The slimy pavement looked like a wet mackintosh. He hurried on towards the left, glancing back now and then to see if he was being followed. In about seven or eight minutes he reached a small shabby house, that was wedged in between two gaunt factories. In one of the top windows stood a lamp. He stopped, and gave a peculiar knock.

The realistic description of an opium den, the prose heightened by Wilde's imaginative colouring of events, is one that has assured Wilde a continued place in cult writing. Dorian's admission of wishing to erase his biography of personal guilt through the autonomous euphoric trance induced by the drug extends to the need to forget those who he has encountered in the night. 'As long as one has this stuff, one doesn't want friends. I think I have had too many friends.' Wilde must have reflected, he must have felt the twist in his nerves as he wrote the latter sentence, for they were all to come back at him, the duplicitous, the mendacious, the corrupt, as he had met them in the night. He would never again be free. Wilde's art demanded life experience, not a complacent settlement for the modified idea of literature. Wilde was never to falter on this issue. He had no intention of renouncing his past in prison; on the contrary, he drew strength from his evolved sense of individuation. In 'De Profundis' he writes: 'To regret one's own experiences is to arrest one's own development. To deny one's own experiences is to put a lie into the lips of one's own life. It is no less than a denial of the soul.' He is arguing quite rightly that we should accept all of our actions, good and bad, as integrants of consciousness and components of a self-monitoring awareness that keeps track of who we are. Memory is like an aeroplane's black box. We may need to listen to the tape after death. And move on.

Saint Oscar and Whitechapel. Dorian visits opium dens as stopping-off places, consoling sites in which he can review his past, either through the time-slowing effects of the drug or through contemplating it naked eye to eye, as one might a wolf as it circles a fire. Wilde treated the night as a mirror for his inner process. In confinement, he recognized suffering inside a double night, the constriction of a cell, and wrote: 'And the remembrance of suffering in the past is necessary to us as the warrant, the evidence, of our continued identity.' And nor is this to deny the Wilde who magnified pleasure, who amplified the moment so as to extract the essence from each nanosecond, writing from prison of his vivid memories of the seasons, and of 'spring always seeming to one as if the flowers had been in hiding, and only came out into the sun because they were afraid that grown-up people would grow tired of looking for them and give up the search'.

What is it we find at the end of the night? Wilde's novel

delights in poetic fascination with the underworld. He chose as his theme what Freud termed the 'return of the repressed', the cyclical preoccupation of his unconscious with his sexuality and his double.

That Wilde was in search of a visionary city, a world radically altered by the senses, is an implicit subtext to *The Picture of Dorian Gray*, a psychic current which invests the novel with apocalyptic potential. Shortly before the book's horrifying denouement, Wilde has Dorian reflect: 'A new life! That was what he wanted. That was what he was waiting for. Surely he had begun it already. He had spared one innocent thing, at any rate. He would never again tempt innocence. He would be good.'

Wilde's only sustained work after his release from prison was 'The Ballad of Reading Gaol', a poem in which he compounded his newly acquired humility and Christian mysticism into the narrative of a fellow prisoner who was to be hanged for murder. Impacted, vicarious, the writing expresses Wilde's own assimilation of a prison ethos through the empathy he felt with a condemned prisoner. Focusing the poem's thrust on the multifarious injustices and brutal inhumanities of the penal system, Wilde, for much of the poem, managed to steer clear of literary affectation and directed his energies towards poetically accentuating all that he found universally intolerable about the system. His new stripped-down style of writing would have been inconceivable without the personal catastrophe that he had undergone to arrive at a more minimally adjectival expression. Of his fellow inmate's crime (the man had been a trooper), Wilde writes:

> He did not wear his scarlet coat,
> For blood and wine are red,
> And blood and wine were on his hands

> When they found him with the dead,
> The poor dead woman whom he loved
> And murdered in her bed.

Wilde fired himself up this one last time to express something of his fall and the demotion of his name to a society scandal. If his language in part found a new flexible sinew it was because Wilde had realized that his own subject matter could be expanded to metabolize ordinary things to counterpoint inherent aesthetic propensities. Through humiliation he had arrived at an acceptance of all experience. He could write about what he would earlier have considered crude and wire it to the poetic imagination's burning current.

> Each narrow cell in which we dwell
> Is a foul and dark latrine,
> And the fetid breath of living Death
> Chokes up each grated screen,
> And all, but Lust, is turned to dust
> In Humanity's machine.

This is Wilde finding a language congruent with his own inner expansion; it's a writing which begins to celebrate freedom from restraint, but it was to be checked by the general debilitation in health and creative impulse that characterized Wilde's last remaining years as an exile in Paris. He had not sufficient time to adjust to a world accelerating towards the twentieth century and to realign his creative energies with the emotional cataclysms that had occurred in his life. It would have taken perhaps a decade for him to have retrieved what was valuable in his work and to have applied that to the volatilized energies liberated by his personal crisis. There's a moving vignette of Wilde in Paris in the last year of his life: as he was crossing the Pont Neuf with Louis Latourette a young woman threw herself into the water, her suicide attempt arrested by a sailor who jumped in to rescue her. Wilde commented:

> I could have rescued that woman, but this act was forbidden me. Yes, it's so. It's horrible. I would have seemed to be seeking attention for myself. Heroism would just have made for scandal. Since my trial, heroism and genius are forbidden me. You've heard how I made a feeble effort to enter a monastery. That would have been the best end. But I would have created a scandal. Pity me. And remember that I could have rescued that woman.

Wilde was, at the time, suffering from the syphilitic degeneration which was to precipitate the encephalitic meningitis from which he was to die. 'I wrote when I did not know life, now that I know the meaning of life, I have no more to write,' he told a friend shortly before he underwent an operation for paracentesis of the eardrum. His nerves disordered by absinthe, Wilde prepared himself for the end with increasingly large cocktails of morphine, opium and champagne. He can have been no more ready for it than any of us, with our inveterate instinctual hopes that we may be exempt from mortality.

SAINT OSCAR
Height: 6 feet
Body-weight: 14½ stone
Eyes: Blue-green
Face: Coarse with rashed vesicles
Hands: Large, 8¼ glove
Feet: Size 10
Disposition: Genius

'But Life, that I had loved so much – too much – has torn me a tiger . . . I am the ruin and wreck of what once was wonderful and brilliant.' A summary of kinds, but this was Saint Oscar who was courageous enough to visit a Paris morgue and review the cold insouciance of the zinc bed that awaited him and irreverent enough to comment: 'My wallpaper and I are fighting a duel to the death. One or the other of us has to go.' Wilde had made so many nights indelible with his inimitably individualistic presence. It may be remembered that Dionysus is a bisexual god, an impulse that governs androgynous consciousness, and Wilde, who was moving psychically towards the integration of male and female, was governed by Dionysian energies. The theatricality of Wilde's emotions were informed by this powerful dominant. And Dionysus was also seen as the enemy of tyrants and as a cult which instigated social change. And as a god who moved under cover of the night.

And of the secret ones who had known Wilde, I like to think they carried memories, not in the sense of sustained reflection but in the jumpy, irregular, intermittent way in which flashbacks score holes in consciousness. I mean those who had known him in the heart of the night and remembered a kindness, a gesture, a ring, an idiosyncratic act composed entirely of his disposition. Their names will never be known, but perhaps a blond-haired young man walked down Regent Street, five years, ten years after Wilde's death, was shocked into immediate recall by the associative memory of a word, an angle of Wilde's face, felt a tear start and disappeared into the crowd.

STRANGE SISTER

for Immaculate

EUGENIO Montale. Nobody ever tells me what colour eyes you had or the name of a shop you visited to buy a mistress lingerie. Was there a small, intimate shop where you chose from La Perla, Pinko or Aubade? The assistant had an idea that you were Montale, but she complied with your conspiratorial sense of secrecy and said nothing.

Nobody ever tells me what colour blue you looked for in choosing shirts or your preference in colognes or what tablets you took for insomnia. Instead I'm offered arid intertextual exegeses of your poems. Your work has become the unlicensed property of academics, and you're not there to prevent them extricating the nerve-roots from lyric.

I think you would have chosen black lingerie for a sultry admirer. You may have done that on the same day as you wrote one of the great poems collected in *The Storm*. The other, the elusive one, the unattainable woman, the strange sister of your poetry, weren't they all facets of an unrealizable love? And she was part of it too, the girl admirer who, without your knowing it and as you crouched to the page, was painting her toenails burgundy in another part of the city. She was blowing on them petulantly before slipping on transparent stockings. And she was in love with your poetry and, even without reading it, the poem you were writing at that moment. Perhaps she shook her hair into a storm as she made a red Cupid's bow with her lipstick, knowing how your poet's instinct was obsessed with retrieving small visual detail. And you as you wrote, contemplated the little black present you would give her later that night. Wasn't it always later for you? The sense that behind the meeting there was night, jackals, the underworld in which the figure of death sat like a singer waiting to go on a stage.

In your poem 'The Storm' the strange sister is the energizing flash, the sudden electrifying shiver of lightning that blasts through all defences. Everything's lit up by her arrival and her presence signals destruction as well as inspired frenzy: 'mad gestures thrown on the air'. Love and hate are one in the dynamic of passion. You must have welcomed the redoubtable metaphysical encounter. This archetype demanded everything from you and, in return, gave you the high drama of the poetic line. The muse or uncompromising sister could only be appeased by the gift of the poem. She goes off into the sky with the histrionic gesture of rucking her hair back in the blazing afterglow of storm and disappears into the dark. She has been 'the fandango's menace' and the pulsating alert of 'tambourines over the blackened pit'. Sister storm. She has no rival in your life. Writing a poem is like being stung by a love-bite. Words burn into the membrane of the unconscious. A poem is the Muse's lipstick imprint an the page. A hot red, a scorching pink.

You go into the kitchen and make coffee. Great poems are absorbed into normal life experience. You wonder if your mother would have been surprised by this one, and anyhow what does it matter? Nobody ever tells me what particular blend of coffee you chose. I imagine it was bitter and had a solid Turkish base. And then the telephone rings and the subject's the weather and the same humid premonition of storm that you've anticipated with such heightened response in the poem. 'It will rain tonight,' your neighbour says, and you: 'The sky's the colour of a girl's nipple.'

You've left the poem out on your desk, and in the same notebook your formidable sister has made other costume changes, other ferocious transmogrifications which have stretched your psyche across the poem's taut energy field. 'I cannot face you nor yet run away,' you've declared in the poem 'On a Letter Unwritten'. The latter poem is expressive of the deep loneliness you feel at all times, a permanent blue mood reflected in your personal mythology as the recurrent image of the sea. Searching for a message in a battle delivered by the wave at Finisterre is your way of insighting the periods in which inspiration is absent. In these dead intervals of waiting, 'Prayer becomes torture, and distraction worse', and there's a nagging sense of incompletion in everything you do. You have to provoke your strange sister into a scene. A poem is a violent scene. It's a confrontation with the inexpressible and it involves blowing fuses on reality. You welcome the stimulus and you fear it. The big high is like orgasm, only the thrusting climax is into an absent body. A poem involves a row with the unconscious, and even the completed work offers no proper resolution but more the organization of fragments into a partial figure. You've put it in other ways. I'm thinking of the ending of 'Personae Separatae':

> You came this way,
> and rested by a heap of lobster-pots,
> then disappeared. In you a light still burns
> above a dark that could be the first day.

And the real woman, Eugenio? What is she doing now? The one you've partly grafted on to the features of your inspirational sister. Poetry is always a sort of cosmetic surgery aimed at creating the ideal woman and yours is never attainable. But the one for whom you've bought the gift of lingerie is out shopping, dodging the cars as she runs for a gap in the sweating traffic to cross the street. Her tight skirt and high heels attract attention from men sitting outside cafés. She throws her head back disdainfully and goes into a delicatessen. She buys cheese, olives and sun-dried tomatoes. And next she purchases stockings. She chooses black silk ones with seams. And because she knows you're thinking of her, she actually feels like the Muse. She has the impression that your poems are written all over her body in violet ink. She believes for a moment that if she pointed a finger towards the lowering clouds she would create lightning and storm. The street would reverberate with crashing thunder and the steaming hiss of rain smoking off cars.

You don't know that she's out shopping and wearing a tight skirt. You've got corrections to make in drafts of other poems. There's that weird one called 'The Eel', in which the metamorphic sister has materialized in still another symbolic disguise. You've got her under your skin. Her protean metaphysicality surprises you by its insidious attempts to attract attention at all costs. You light a cigarette and blow smoke into her invisible face. And nobody's ever told me what brand of cigarettes you smoked. Nobody's made the connection between the smoke you inhaled and the inferno-glow of your poems. Your strange sister always arrived on fire. Her ignition of your brain chemistry caused you almost to autocombust in the process of writing.

Your inspirer arriving as a Luciferean eel was another big event. Perhaps you looked at the label sewn into black silk and read La Perla, assuring yourself that the recipient of this gift would warm to its aesthetic appeal as well as its potential for provocation. The telephone again.

You've left a book at a café. The sky's now turned the bruised colour of a magnolia petal. You can almost smell the storm twitching in the ionized atmosphere. You pour another cup of coffee. The black silk is starting to crackle with jumpy electricity. What's it you've written of 'The Eel,' that flashes into our faces as a blinding presentiment of being destroyed by the other, the vengeful sister?

> the spark that says
> everything begins when everything seems
> the black char of a buried stump;
> the brief rainbow, a twin
> to the other set in your forehead
> which sparkles brilliantly among
> generations immersed in mud, can you
> not take her for a sister?

Here the volatilized sister is both a destructive and a redemptive force. She's burnt you to a charred stump, a metaphorical extinction, but that was necessary so that you would be reborn. The poet dies each time he experiences close contact with the sister's awesome eyes. You know also that a rainbow is born from the conflict, a brief iridescent dazzle of vapour that confirms the bridge that the imagination builds between unconscious and conscious worlds. You know all about that, Eugenio, for your poems are a triumph of the concretely symbolic over an abstrusely hermetic inner dialogue. They affirm the possibility of the other becoming a reality. The strange sister coming out of the crowd as a woman with feline eyes and a livid statement of red lipstick drawing attention to her untouchable presence.

I like to think that your major poems like 'The Storm', 'Dora Markus', 'Little Testament' and the vampishly malevolent 'The Eel' entered real time as pressurized deliveries after a long period of gestation in inner space. I tell myself that you were prepared for them. The woman in your heart at the time, for whom you had bought the delicate black silk panties, was the closest to the embodiment of an archetype that you could manage. She was, at the time of your looking out for rain, about to turn the key in the lock of her apartment and deposit her food purchases in the fridge.

You're preoccupied with re-evaluating the eel's journey against the current, its snaky migration through streams from Apennine rocks to the Romagna. You've spent a lot of time in your life looking into standing and running water. This eel is 'torch, whiplash' and 'earthly love arrow'. Its passage towards a completed destiny is irreversible. It can endure droughts and survive. You've conjured up a psychic force that, more than storm, can blow the lights in your apartment. And what do you do with the poem now that it's written? It can't be converted into money or anything else but itself. But you have an idea that your storm will live on and travel down the centuries.

Nobody ever tells me what sort of aperitif you savoured in the early evening. Was it Punte Mes? Did you brick the glass up with ice as a prelude to uncorking the wine? And nobody ever tells me if you preferred red or white. What was the region that sat best on your palate?

And as a co-extension of your idiosyncratic human needs, there's the serious work of the poem. It's an organism that exists because of you, and yet, at the same time, you've only its earthing-point. You've spent maybe a few hours with something that has always existed in the archetypal unconscious. You've given the poem a valency that belongs to your own modern times, and that's the stamp of your individual genius. That's why you're Eugenio Montale. The ability to energize images is coded into your biology. Sometimes you'd prefer to be looking at girls in minimal bikinis on the Ligurian coast, and then the serious gift that you carry starts up on red alert. Imaginative tension drives you to take refuge in words, those dense, constellated clusters of language that comprise your poems and which look like the geography of poetry itself, a map hacked from the exact interchange of inner and outer realities.

You drink your coffee, flick through the pages of Italian *Vogue* and return to making an overview of some of the recent poems you have been inspired to write. Your pouting admirer is sitting on her bed, adjusting the stockings she has bought to the tautness of black suspender straps. The silk breathes weightlessly on her legs. She likes the way her burgundy toenails show alluringly through each toepoint. She's imagining herself in ways that she hopes you'll see her. You keep on in your blue halo of smoke, wondering how you've managed all of your writing life to transform the ordinary into the exalted. The physical coastline that you know so well has become in your poetry a reverential metaphysical arena over which absolutes contend. Nobody ever tells me if you drove a car or what make or colour it was or if you flashed around town in it. You would have played music in the car and would have worn black sunglasses.

And your 'Coastguard's House'. I like to think the place was an imaginary construct, a house you built to shelter the poet. He could hang out there, observing the blue and green drag of the tides, while you were in the cafés doing nothing in particular. And that solitary, storm-blasted, salt-eroded shack would also be inhabited by your strange sister. It was her den. She would be alone there 'breathless in the spinning dark'. She'd be going mad in there, until her wild, importunate screams drove you to write the poem. Poems occurred for you on days when the strange sister got leave from her asylum and had business with you. And your way of responding was to take up that grave, melancholic tone of attempting to constrain the Muse's hysteria. And you did it masterfully.

Your coastguard's house is perched above a vertical drop to the breakers. Surf boils over the inshore reefs. You'd probably sighted just such a place along the coast, and in time it grew to be the patent symbol of one of your great poems. And there's that moment in the poem when the light comes through, and it's the red light of a petrol tanker trudging across a shifting skyline. There's no lonelier image in poetry than that excruciating moment when the ship's light shows redly through the haze. It's an image that enforces your isolation as a poet. There was no other way of sharing the experience except through the medium of poetry. Everything you'd wanted to say about the poet's role as an outsider, and his despair at feeling excluded from the social fabric, came together in those four stanzas. 'You don't remember our jagged outpost,/or which of us remains, and which goes lost.' There's a terminal sadness here that suggests you knew all along that the strange sister would never enter into any form of stable relationship with you. When she wants you to write, she bites you and kicks up chaos in your unconscious. What you get is an inconsolable longing for her as a real woman. And because she can never truly become physical, you are condemned to keep on reinvoking her through poetry. You even begin 'The Coastguard's House' on a note of bitter resignation: 'You don't recall the coastguard's house.' She's that hard. A bitch of a strange sister.

The Muse never attends her casualties. She will have poets die of poverty, she will leave them heartbroken, tormented or mad, and the only trace of her having existed is a whiff of nocturnally pungent Shalimar. The strange sister wears Guerlain perfumes, just like your Milanese admirer who is aligning the seams of her stockings in a mirror. She unstops the bottle and applies Shalimar behind her knees. It's now a quarter to eight, and a slow stop-and-start rain has moved in over town.

You pour yourself out a glass of wine. The magnolia leaves are being dented by rain. Splotchy, abrasive notes of rain. And there's that other fizzy achievement, 'Little Testament', to cause you concern as you thumb through your notebook. This poem is another of your stories about getting burnt by your sister's monsooning temperament. This time she's represented as a 'tempestuous Lucifer' who alights on a ferry's prow 'in the Thames, Hudson, or the Seine'. She's the destroying angel 'breathless with news that now's the time'. Her power to possess you is greater than yours to resist. What you hold on to are tokens of a trust that you'll not only survive her renewed assault but convert the metaphorical wounds she's inflicted on you into a sign, a universal hope that the poem is still a viable channel affording redemption. She won't let go of you, nor you of her. You've compounded her rainbow, her corresponding symbol occurs in 'The Eel' into a granulated powder to be kept in a compact. I like the way you are intimate with a woman's little things that she keeps in a handbag. Poets need to be familiar with a strange sister's cosmetic accoutrements. And you tell us you really know the score this time:

> The sign was right: he who saw it
> can never miss you again.
> Each knows his own: pride
> was not flight: humility was not misplaced; the brief catch
> of a flame struck down there, was from no match.

And you impart other truths that come of being bitten: 'a story endures in ash/and persistence is only extinction' – you keep things in lower case, and so do I. How we hate those poets who pronounce every line with a redundant capital. 'Each knows his own,' you affirm, and there's no question about that. Strange sisters gravitate to lyric poets. Even burnt to ash, the poet resurrects in a fury of blazing nerves. And I'm sure, Eugenio, if there had been an autopsy conducted on your dead body 'Little Testament' would have been written an the walls of your heart. It would have been needled there by the notch-narks of teeth.

But the absence, the inseparable void that could never be filled by the strange sister, was of course the desperation that drove you to write. You could leave her a bottle of Shalimar on the rocks, place it high up above the tides and hope she would retrieve it. And the admirer who's already growing anxious that you are late for the dinner she is in the process of preparing leaves a different sort of pang in your heart. You'd like her to be everything to you, but she's human and will never fulfil your total needs. She has a real life independent of yours. She buys food, stockings, household cleaners, magazines, hair-dyes and books from a nearby stationer's. She also loves your poetry and reads it when she slumps into a downmood. But on bad days she would rather go to a movie than puzzle over your enigmatic longing for an imaginary woman. She wonders why she can't be everything to you. You're always so blue and travelling to the coast to reacquaint yourself with stormy waters. You tell her you go out there in search of inspiration. What you're really looking for are rainbows. A vaporous pink and green eyebrow shows up on unpredictably squally days. You know it's her sign, the bridge on which she waits for you, disclosing the seven veils of an ethereal stripper. You throw out your arms in response, and the first lines of a poem are already tumbling into your head. That's the closest you'll get to her, and it hurts.

As when
you turned and with your hand rucked back
a cloud of hair –
greeted me to step off into the dark.
Your sister's high salute, like a woman stepping out of her dress, and
daring the man to follow. Daring him to burn.

You're now driving across the city to your rendezvous. The excitement, the anticipation you had felt all day at the prospects of an evening spent with your vivaciously shock-haired mistress are beginning to be replaced by a feeling of unsettling disappointment. The strange sister's started to antagonize you by feeding lines into your head. Your compulsive loyalty has you want to swing the car around in a flurry of headlights and return home. Nobody ever tells me if you wore neckties in the evening and, if so, what colour you thought was suitable to impress a young woman. Nobody ever tells me where you bought those ties and if you knew the assistant personally. They would have been silk neckties in various shades of blue and green.

And anyhow, you decide to turn back or, better still, head for the sea. You'll telephone from a bar overlooking the coast. You need to see red and green coastal lights and speculate on the destination of a ship pushing its wake out into the dark. How many broken hearts has it left behind?

Now you feel better, and you don't. This time you need a hard-hitting Scotch. Your strange sister has entered you with disruptive chaos. And wouldn't you do it all over again? Love her all over again, baby blue.

THE ANGEL IN POETRY

Who, if I cried, would hear me in the angels'
hierarchies? and even if one of them forced
me suddenly to his heart, I would be consumed
by his overwhelming presence. For beauty's nothing
but the beginning of terror, we're hardly able to bear,
and we're fascinated because it serenely disdains
to destroy us. Every angel's terrible.

RILKE'S invocation at the beginning of the *Duino Elegies* to what appears to be a dispassionate intermediary, a hieratic intercessor on the angelic plane, gives voice to the profound dilemma of loss and psychic anguish that he experienced both in his isolation as a poet and in the agonized arena of his psyche as an existential being. Rilke was, to use his own terms, always in the process of becoming. He waited for the word as one waits for a lover to return. In the case of the *Duino Elegies* and their inspired inception, he claimed that the voice had arrived on 21 January 1912 when, in an agitated state, he had gone out to walk on the battlements at Duino and been surprised by a big wind: the Bora.

From the Vedic hymns to the films of Jean Cocteau and Wim Wenders, the angel has come to stand for dualism, for the schizoid components of psyche in which death is countered by resurrection and the unsublimated wound by its transformative counterpart of healing. Death, as a psychological state, gains expansive form and content through the imagination. One might say that death and the imagination are interchangeable, for post-biological frontiers are the speculative subject of so much of our inner questioning, and the topology we give to death is in direct proportion to how we imagine it. If angels are seen as aspects of light, imploded constellations interfaced in our neurologies, then they are also recognized for their underworld capacities – the black angel who points the way to destruction, representing a negative valency in that dualistic hierarchy. In Rilke's words: 'Every angel's terrible.' There is sometimes an inconsolable apprehension to the configurative possibilities inherent in life which seems to negate even the idea of redemption. We can be beaten flat by a commitment to life which is also a responsibility to death.

Rilke's 'First Elegy' begins on a note of abandonment and colours according to the tonal shades of his questioning. His own deep sense of human loneliness becomes translated into compassionate empathy with the great lovers, losers and those who died young. Out of restless disquiet his voice shifts from image to image in the attempt to find an affirmative resting point:

> And so I hold myself back and bite hard
> on my choked cry. Ah, who can we turn to
> in our need? Not angels, not humans,
> and already the animals are aware
> that we're not really at home
> in our interpreted world. And perhaps there remains for us
> some tree on a hillside, which every day
> arrests the eye. And there stays with us yesterday's street
> and the loyalty of a perfect habit
> that moved in and would never give up its hold.

Rilke's crisis, and where he finds himself at the time of writing, is that neither angels nor humans appear to offer propitiation for the hunted state of his psyche. Consolation is to be found in the incidental habits of living and in the comfort afforded by the familiar vision of a tree located on a hillside. We may remember that Rimbaud, engaged in the passionate spiritual combat of writing *A Season in Hell*, remarks in his state of outraged hyper-dissociation: 'A hard night. Dried blood smokes on my face, and nothing lies behind me but that antagonistic little tree. The fight for the soul is as brutal as warfare; but the sight of justice is God's pleasure alone.'

Rilke, whose experiences in Paris had crystallized into the spectrum of pathological neuroses described in the *Notebooks of Malte Laurids Brigge*, had quit his flat in the rue de Varenne in October 1911 and at the invitation of Princess Marie had come to live in the castle at Duino. Finding himself alone there, he was forced inward to an imaginal interior, a locus he both dreaded and anticipated with fascinated compulsion. The poet is always placed in the position of debating whether or not to open Pandora's Box. This gold box buried in the underworld is the repository of images and the mysteries surrounding love and death. It's opened at the risk of madness. The poet retreats with a fistful of images and counts out his precious stones. And each time he returns there's the same sense of redoubtable prohibition surrounding the act. Rilke at Duino was burnt. He was in discourse with the sub-textual display in his unconscious. The neural angels were black and belonged to the syndrome of delusional paranoia. Rilke wrote to Princess Maria:

Loneliness is a true elixir, it forces the disease completely to the surface; first one has to get bad, worse, worst . . . then, though, one gets well. I creep about for the whole day in the thickets of my life and scream like a savage and clap my hands: – you wouldn't believe what hair-raising creatures then fly up.

Rilke, who regarded psychoanalysis as an unwelcome 'disinfection of the soul' and who preferred to transmute free-radical obsessions into the synchronous phenomena of poetry, made a reflective study of his exaggerated fears. 'If my devils were driven out,' he confided in a letter, 'my angels also would receive a slight shock, and, you see, I cannot risk that at any price.' We can argue that the angel is an agent of anxiety, as well as a messenger we sometimes mistake for a hitch-hiker who materializes beside the road on the long drive across a continent. And angels, as Rilke realized them, were part of the everyday encounters in his life. The experiential awakenings occasioned by being in the presence of a lover, together and apart, and of realizing one's own death and the death of others and of coming into contact with the immediately marvellous were all intuitive impulsions towards contact with a sublimated other.

There are days when we go out into the blue afternoon or into the night and meet the perfect stranger. We don't know why he or she happened to be there at that particular moment or why we intersected in time. There's the feeling that the person has dropped in from the sky or has suddenly materialized as a complementarity to our needs – and often this is the beginnings of love. We walk out into the rain with the stranger, and everything lights up gold. It seems like we've known our counterpart for ever, and perhaps we have. And all night, subsequent to the next date, we lie awake reviewing our past like a film fast-forwarded into the future. Suddenly everything that was buried is retrievable; there's so much light inside the head we feel illuminated. We have entered a time-slip and know the angel.

If the angels for Rilke embodied a sense of absence which existed in his psyche, then for him poetry was a way of searching for the idea of completion through invoking pure being. The thrust of the 'First Elegy', its drive unit, is towards attempting to arrest the unattainable, and then finding consolation in turning away each time to a resigned state of celebratory failure. The analogy with the lover is pertinent here. In time the perfect stranger will grow to be demystified: the initial carbonated fizz of meeting will graduate to a settling in, a humanizing of the relationship. The magic may not disappear, but perhaps the lover will turn into a stranger again and we will come back one day to an empty flat, a letter, a sense of too much space in the room and a cry of desertion will rise to the throat. Rilke's great truths are established through disappointment. Apart from his early and short-lived marriage to Clara Westhoff Rilke lived most of his life alone and in search of an ideal spiritual companion who would accord with his work. He developed an obedience to solitude; but he left a door to himself open should the anticipated one arrive. Do angels leave footprints in the shape of stars, or do they materialize through psychic visualization in a relationship of contact to contactee? For consolation Rilke looked to the great lovers and particularly to those who had been broken. By way of assuagement to his damaged nerves he pitches his tone to that of being an accomplice to the universal theme of loss and unrequited love:

> When longing hits you, sing of great lovers;
> their famous passions need more exposure,
> and of women deserted, the ones you envy,
> who would love you more than the gratified.
> Begin again. Try out your impossible praise again;
> remember the hero lives on: even his fall
> was only a pretext for another birth.

The affirmative note here has the abandoned women appear

like angels sitting in a café at the end of the world. Perhaps they are listening to albums by Billie Holiday, to songs like 'Gloomy Sunday', 'Solitude' and 'I Cover the Waterfront', the lyrics given a blue rinse by the subjective melancholy informing the voice. It's the poet who lives on as the apotheosized hero, for the line has grown to be autonomous, and it will live independent of its creator.

We conceive of angels as signifiers of light. They are the illuminati who constellate the dark. My mention of Billie Holiday is not without significance, for the songs of unrequited love interpreted by women singers, and most notably by torch singers, are also an expression of the diva or the angel. The singer lights a torch in the heart which has remained constant, despite betrayal. It is that impassioned flourish of emotive light which colours a torch singer's repertoire. It is interesting to note in this respect that the Sanskrit word *deva* means 'shining one' or 'luminous being'. Today the torch singer, or diva, may dress in sequins to accommodate that role and continues under the spotlight to act out the histrionics of a fallen angel.

The plaintively elegiac folk poem 'When I Was a Young Man' often forms the basis for improvised lyrics by torch singers. In Marc Almond's rendition of the song we encounter the line 'I want six young angels to carry my coffin.' The lamenting youth, anticipating his death, requests that they place a bunch of white roses on his body. The lyric suggests that the angels, who are also the pall-bearers, are propitiatory guardians of the young libertine after his death; they are drawn to him because of the waywardness in his life and will now lead the repentant into the halls of death.

Rilke's necromantic obsession with the dead and with their retrieval through the neural network generated by inspirational charge was the predominant theme of his work. He believed in returning death to life. He saw the death-state as a receptor in the mind that we had purposely closed down. He considered that absence could be healed by reconciliation with death. And the *Duino Elegies*, in their shifts of argument, their affirmative lyric flights and in their attempts to redress the issues of the desperate need to know love and to companion death are a movement towards universal consolation for the solitary. Rilke risks going so far inward in his undertaking that we continue to rediscover his findings according to the reconstitution of psyche. It's what allows the *Elegies* to appear modern nearly a century after their composition. A poetry that contracts on the imagination runs the risk of being deleted by time. The imaginally expansive is under constant psychological reclamation. Or as Rilke has it: 'Who speaks of winning: survival is all.'

Angels, in their poetic and iconic embodiment, appear to inhabit a parallel universe. The addition of wings connects them to the principle of verticality, and, on a metaphoric level, this uplift implies a function which surpasses normal states of consciousness. We experience flight in our dreams. Unconscious energies allow us to lift off in the gravity-free domain of inner space. In the final pages of J.G. Ballard's extraordinarily futuristic novel *The Unlimited Dream Company* the entire inhabitants of a village fly off into the sky. Our preoccupation with flight through aeronautical technology and space travel has confirmed the scientific reality of our inner dream. In all altered states, and I include the writing of poetry as such a phenomenon, the desire is to go beyond the self. The poet burns on over reach.

Rilke spent most of his life in a state of nervous terror. He wrote to Lou Salome:

There are days when I look at the whole of creation with the fear that some agony may break out in it and cause it to scream, so great is my fear of the abuse which the body, in so many things brings on the soul, which finds peace in the animals and safety only in the angels.

And here is a little story. The poet walks out at the end of a late-Septemberish afternoon. He's been alone all day at his work. Interruptions, telephone calls, faxes, none of these have succeeded in intruding on his distracted state of consciousness. Dissociation is, for him, a natural way of being. When he hits the street it's like affiliating with a parallel universe. Squashy, toad-mottled leaves are down on the pavement, their patterns face up on the concrete like an inventive mosaic of tattoos. There's a bronze underside to a rainy indigo sky. The poet moves through a succession of streets, window-shopping, eye-shopping, looking at incidental detail – but following mostly the impulsive direction of his inner dictates. He's walking the same road as the poem. If he telescopes towards the part of town where stairs drop to the river he feels he may have some orientation towards a directive. The light in the sky appears to be on dimmers. Vertical rays pour out of a wall of dark blue cumulus. He takes comfort in thinking that the rain will come on with the dark.

As he catdrops a level to the river's slick skin, a ferry travelling downstream showing red and green lights, he sights a figure dressed in silver walking away from him. It's as though his eyes turn the person round, and the response is immediate. All of the waiting and patience in him has found a reciprocal attraction. What he has imagined in dreams, in missing time, in trance states, in intervals of disorientation and dissociation, has materialized as a reality. The sighting frequency in his nerves has made contact. The light coming off the river is like a hologram on his skin. In the pre-dark the figure walking towards him could be a drop-in or an angel. That sort of light surrounding someone denotes an extra-biological neurology.

As the figure approaches so a gateway opens in his vision. Past and future are synchronously immediate. A smell comes back from his childhood. It's of the musty apples which used to be piled in a glass fruit bowl on the kitchen table. What have apples got to do with Mars or any of the billions of stars in the galaxy where this figure in silver may have evolved? Time no longer exists. The sensory association to be made with apple smells isn't so much as part of his history, more as an awareness which is continuously now. The figure nearing him also wears silver glasses. There's no eye contact. There's only the realization that this had to happen. The poet's about to call out when the weightless body walks clean into and through him. What is there in place of the silver are words as visual entities lighting up behind the eyes. The poet assimilates the illuminated register of words. He reads in the blinding flash: Perfect love is to have known and not to have kept the unattainable. Each time you write you recreate me. I am the distance you meet on the page. I am that star.

Meetings by the river. Rimbaud kicking about a barn in the dog-days of August 1873. The place is set back from the main house at Roche. The emotional cataclysms surrounding his tempestuous relationship with Paul Verlaine have resulted in the latter's being imprisoned in Brussels for having shot Rimbaud through the wrist. The youth, for Rimbaud still hasn't reached the age of twenty, has returned home to recount his experiences of combat, both with the daemon of poetry and its personification in the person of Verlaine, whom Rimbaud called the 'infernal bridegroom'. Rimbaud's experience of the angel is far more demonstratively physical than Rilke's. His struggle is a brutal one to affirm light over dark. The resultant prose poem, *A Season in Hell*, gives the impression that the poet has fought with his daemon. Rimbaud

speaks of delirious raving. In the attempt to go beyond himself
Rimbaud hypes his chemistry to a state of hallucinated receptivity. Rimbaud's incandescent agony is like a whip cut across the
face of received poetry. He rarely accepts the given line but coun-
terpoints its arrival with an urgency to shift it higher up the
visionary scale. And in order to undertake the struggle, he set
himself apart like a shaman. His sister tells us that he remained
locked away for days fighting for the stormy eloquence which
became his poem. He was also attempting to dispossess himself of
the black angel, Paul Verlaine, whose inimical shadow had seeped
into his psyche. The poem asks for the interchange of exorcism
with possession by light. A process of redemptive alchemy. 'One
sees one's own angel, never someone else's angel,' he writes from
the flaming heart of the poem, affirming, as always, the powerful
sense of individuation which is an integral part of the creative
thrust. Rimbaud is probably the most singularly perverse and
contrary of visionary poets, and he is that because he receives his
hard-won vision like a child disdainfully throwing away gifts and
then asking for more. Rilke works with the grain of the poem and
Rimbaud against it. For Rimbaud, in the act of writing, death of
the ego is impossible; he attacks the work for coming to him.
Rilke receives and celebrates the source. Rimbaud's struggle is at
all times intolerable: he would like to relinquish his poetic commitment, but his fear of the ordinary, or what he dismissively calls
'work', is greater than his fear of dismemberment as a shaman.
Nearing the end of the cosmographic trip his poem has described,
for Rimbaud is an imaginal cosmogonist, his violent mood-swings
oscillate between temporal rebellion and spiritual optimism.
Rilke's self-contained agony never devolves into the self-derision
with which Rimbaud attacks himself. Rimbaud ruthlessly points
a gun at himself:

Here I recognize my rotten upbringing. What of it! . . . I'll be twenty, if the others are going to be twenty . . . No! At this moment I rebel against death. Work seems too trivial to my pride: my betrayal of myself to the world would be too minor a torment. At the last moment I should strike out, right and left . . .

Rimbaud's rightful hatred of work, which subjugates the individual to the system, is of course an energy experienced by all those who resent being de-individualized by corporate ideologies. The child is free to dream in a psychic space in which inner and outer are not clearly separated. The abandonment of that state at the crisis surrounding puberty is usually matched in the non-creative sensibility by an awakening to the responsibilities of a career and social integration. The poet can accept neither of these things without seriously compromising his gift. Rimbaud says he would strike out, he would oppose captivity. What he looks toward is a world in which imagination becomes reality. Rimbaud writes:

From the same desert, in the same night, always my tired eyes awaken to the silver star, without disturbing the three kings of life, the three magi – the heart, the soul, the mind. When shall we journey, beyond the beaches and the mountains, to salute the beginnings of the new work, the new age, the rout of tyrants and demons – the end of superstition; to adore – as the first to know it – Christmas on earth.

Rimbaud's angels are the agents of the new world. If Rilke's angels are distinctly personal, as well as being universal archetypes, then Rimbaud's are often aspected in the light of being avengers. Because Rimbaud's combat is so much in the immediate, his method is one of direct attack. He treats the line he's handling like a snake. By way of contrast Rilke's experience may be seen as psychologically reflected or encountered with a mediating defence mechanism that shields him from getting burnt. The ferocity of Rimbaud's shamanic confrontation with his daemon suggests the idea of wrestling with an angel. There is sweat, torment and, in Rimbaud's case, bloodshed, self-inflicted wounds as the consequence of somatizing the visitant. 'Dried blood smokes on my face,' he tells us. He is exhausted by the assault of an enervating delirium:

> My health was threatened. Terror lived in me. I fell into sleeps which lasted several days, and when I awoke, continued in the saddest dreams. I was ripe for death, and my vulnerability led me by way of a dangerous road to the edge of the world and to Cimmeria, an underworld for shadows and whirlwinds.

Jung said: 'If angels are anything at all, they are personified transmitters of unconscious content that are seeking expression.' The poet attracts or embodies the angel by way of connecting with synchronous events and through himself acting as an intermediary for epiphanic illumination. Rimbaud's imperative, 'Now's the time of the ASSASSINS', would have us know that angels are also terrorists; their insurrectionist capacities will subvert the social order in the interests of expanding the frontiers of the imagination. Rimbaud's hope of bringing about significant changes in the way we experience the universe, through the infiltrating agents of poetry, smacks of the visionary courage of those who risk disintegration in the course of channelling transformative energies. There's no easy way through or out of such a conquest and Rimbaud, in spite of his extreme poverty and social impotence, furthered the continuous dream we have of the heavenly city: 'Christmas on earth'.

That we read Rilke and Rimbaud as part of a poetic angelology is due to the changes effected by their poetry. Rilke's premonitory line, 'You must change your life', has set up a psychological resonance which has reverberated throughout our century. His self-challenging assertion has grown to be the premise from which modern psychology operates. We demand more of the poem than a social conscience. We ask that it turns us round, so that we gain an insight into the marvellous that's inherent in the ordinary. In the 'Eighth Elegy' Rilke pronounces our discomfort with living, our apprehension that 'we live our lives forever taking leave'. We're wrongly orientated, and the poem, when it is rightly directed, compensates for the imbalance:

Who's turned us round like this,
so that no matter what we do, we seem
about to go away? Just as a man stood on the last hill above his valley
one last time, turns, stops, looks back –
so we live, forever taking leave.

Rilke confirmed his beliefs in an art that goes beyond its creator's reserves, as he wrote to his wife: 'Works of art are always the products of a danger incurred, of an experience pursued to the end, to the point where man can no longer continue.' For the visionary poet the continuity is resumed by a future generation that intersects with the work's arrival. For poems go on arriving like the Big Bang. If the universe was once, as it seems probable, compressed into a space less than a fraction of a centimetre in radius before it blew into the eruptive star-glow of the galaxies, then the experience from which a poem is derived is similarly compacted in the unconscious and quantized through the autonomous split-off into language. A poem lights up with the glow of its quantum expansion.

In medieval paintings we see a contemplative Virgin, often reading a book, being impregnated through the ear by an angel. Gold, angelic semen. This would suggest that listening, by which I mean attunement to the big silences of inner space, is the way of attracting inspiration or its personified carrier, the angel. Don't we all listen for a voice or a sign to point the way forward? At times of change or crisis within our lives we remain silent. The Virgin attracts the angel because she is prepared to receive. The poet attracts the poem because he is listening out. The go-between, or angel, carries a psychosexual message. Something will be born because of the contact. The Virgin gives birth to the Word as flesh; she incarnates the Logos. The poet, at an inspired prompting, sets about retrieving from the unconscious something he knows but has forgotten.

There are days when we need to be completely alone and in that solitude embrace silence. And sometimes we may hear a voice say our name when we're out shopping, busy in the crowd, as much as we may hear it spoken on a deserted beach with blue sea-fog blanking out the horizon. Who was it that called? Ourselves? Or someone reminding us that we're never quite alone? When we're listening right, we do change our lives. We start to feel the anticipation and the excitement of being in love with the unknown. Days later, or weeks or months, we encounter the perfect stranger. It may happen on a train journey, in a café, at a party or simply walking down the street. We attract because we have set in motion the ability to receive. And this is what falling in love and writing poetry share in common. Lovers find themselves wanting to write or read poetry, as a complementarity act to their altered state. Love has had them break through to a space where angels visit. The unconscious is suddenly full of stars.

Leonard Cohen's poem 'The Stranger Song', on the album *Songs of Leonard Cohen*, is a profound mystic evocation of contact with a go-between. The stranger here is an arrival or angel who will never surrender to conditional love. He will always occupy a place one stage further than the need addressed to him. The poem, or song, is full of that ambiguous longing for a union with the other or the grief aspect of psyche which so characterizes Cohen's work:

> But now another stranger seems to want you to ignore his
> dreams, as though they were the burden of some other.
> You've seen that man before, his golden arm dispatching
> cards, but now it's rusted from the elbow to the finger.
> And he wants to trade the game he plays for shelter. He
> wants to play the game he knows for shelter.

Here we have the image of a fallen angel: 'You've seen that man before, his golden arm dispatching cards, but now it's rusted from the elbow to the finger.' But though the stranger gives the appearance of searching for asylum and of wishing to remain incarnate he is unable to stay or to offer anything else but unrequited love for his human contactee. The result is a disappointed longing, despite the immanence surrounding the encounter:

> And leaning on your window-sill,
> he'll say one day you caused his will
> to weaken with your love and warmth and shelter.
> And then taking from his wallet an old schedule of trains
> he'll say, 'I told you when I came I was a stranger.'

Another experience of love. We lose because the other person has no wish to be tied to a commitment. He or she is passing through. It may be that love in this context has no wish to hurt and so remains detached. And for the poet, the inspirational visitant comes and goes, incites the process and departs. The poet, in the act of writing, suffers the loss of the inspired angel. The gift is implanted, but the autonomous work must follow. The poet is out on his own. The angel who delivered through the ear is now on a return trajectory through inner space. The poem is established in the afterglow of that light. If the visitant were to stay there would be nothing of the tension engendered by separation. It is what we don't have that inspires in us the need to create. Cohen's poems and songs are full of bitter-sweet longing. He is happy in his need and sad in his gain. Disinherited by his fall, our fall, from a state of completion, he celebrates the state of disinheritance which is the creative domain. Cohen's work may be seen as part of the continuous invocation of the mystic other, and its manifestation through the sexual energies of love. Cohen's melancholy, with his dark blue baritone delivery, has been a source of consolation to wounded lovers, an aural panacea, ever since his voice broke cover in the sixties. I would call his novel *Beautiful Losers* one of the most sublime erotico-spiritual epiphanies in twentieth-century fiction.

I want to discuss singing and, more specifically, the image of the torch singer. The torch singer is sometimes referred to as a diva, an angel, or simply a star – all references to the angelified presence in the impassioned voice. Singing to redeem, singing to die. And I'm indebted in my reading to a fine passage of voice exegesis in Therese Schroeder-Shekers' essay, 'The Material Half of the Angel', in which she writes:

> The greatest singing takes place when we observe periods of silence. You cannot talk or sing all the time and still expect to have something mean-

ingful to give away. This observation of silence is crucial in identifying the split between concert artist and concert audience. A fragmentation exists; the two are asking to be one, but this is difficult to achieve. Silence is the key; our own inner silence must be allowed to be heard by the audience. We heal that split by transforming stage into altar and by an exteriorized performance into a vital, streaming inner life that is made available, audible, to others.

The idea of the stage as an altar, or sacral precinct, is of course exactly that which imparts a sense of awe to the performer. He or she is set apart by reason of being receptive to breath and externalizing emotion through voice. Torch singing's about giving form to an internal storm. Emotion at the interior is channelled through the hyoid bone by units of breath. Singing is also about empathizing with somebody else's story. If she is performing someone else's song, the singer must enter deeply into a narrative which will most likely tell the story of an unrequited love, or of a pain the voice will rewrite in order to affirm hope in suffering. And for the three or four minutes of the song's duration time is suspended for the audience. We listen and enter so deeply into the silence we have prepared for ourselves in order to listen that we hear and receive. Ordinary hearing, by which I mean our editing in and out of noise and our concentration on what is being said, is an imperfect way of listening. It is listening with impaired receptivity. Faced with the confrontational image of the diva on stage, her torch flaming in her heart, we relive pockets of timelessness. The time-free zone that exists in the act of writing a poem involves losing awareness of chronology. A trance state or autonomous flow takes over. Where was I all those hours? Somewhere else. I would say, in the stars.

When we leave the diva's concert we're so distracted that we can't account for where we've been. We walk outside to a street which appears altered. We are changed, because the pain we conceal has found its correspondence in the diva's repertoire. I may go home and dream of angels. They inhabit, in the title of an old song, 'The House of the Rising Sun'. And who has not felt the presence of angels in listening to Aretha Franklin sing:

> Gotta find me an angel to fly away with me
> Gotta find me an angel, who would set me free
> A heart without a home I don't want to be alone.
> Gotta find me an angel: in my life.

Time-slips, or missing time, bring another extraterrestrial voyager to look in through the cosmic window. It's the figure of the alien, the humanoid, the mutant, the walk-in, which has assumed increasing importance to late-twentieth-century culture. The alien, like the angel, is personified in the likeness of a human. We feel able to establish contact with interplanetary travellers who are in search of ecosystems which generate a species identifiable to their own. Jung described the UFO as the sending in by the self of something to land in the unconscious. Ufonaut overflights, and the countless sightings reported by attuned percipients, suggest that the UFO phenomenon is a part of angelology. Close-encounter experiences, sometimes involving abductees who are mentally and biologically researched by their extraterrestrial counterparts, have become a significant part of the collective unconscious experience. As with the visitation of the angel, so the alien enters through a gateway in the receptive individual. Sometimes the trauma surrounding contact leads to the contactee having to undergo regression hypnosis in order fully to evaluate the psychological implant left by extraterrestrial entry.

We should remember Rilke's line: 'Every angel's terrible.' The way in is not without disturbance. The meeting of two parallel worlds, the angel and the human, the alien and the contactee, lead to implosive volatility. There's suddenly somebody in one's space who shouldn't be there but who has found a way in. If an intruder breaks into one's home, it's an external event. He comes through a window or a door and his physical body is situated in external space. With the alien, possession may come on the inside and then materialize to exterior contact. The arrival may enter through a dream and on the sleeper's awakening be translated into a reality.

Often aliens angels are described as small, usually about four feet tall, and with the distinguishing characteristic of prominent wraparound eyes. That almost all data about UFOs is subjected to a process of disinformation by governments is part of the cover-up designed to conceal the existence of extraterrestrial life. That certain minds are attuned to alien contact seems no less implausible than the receptivity which attracts angels or the channelled inspiration which directs the writing of poetry. When UFOs materialize they cause electromagnetic interference: car headlights and engines stop, the percipient may experience intense body heat and strong feelings of dissociation. The whole ambience surrounding contact is surely little different to the mystic response of those visited by angels. Both happenings involve an awakening which is also terror.

Are UFOs physical presences or are they, as Jung supposed, manifestations of the unconscious? Jung's view that a flying saucer is a symbolic messenger is upheld by Robert Sardello, who proposes that 'a UFO is not a physical object, but something making an appearance in the physical, at the threshold'. Sardello sees UFOs as thrones or structures which create physical matter rather than as the metallic, discoid objects we imagine them to be.

In 1947, witnesses at Corona in New Mexico claimed to have seen a saucer crash on a flight path over the Magdalena/San Mateo Mountains after having been hit either by lightning or some kind of anti-aircraft projectile. A great quantity of wreckage was blown out across the Corona desert before the debris was subjected to the normal disinformative process. Ufological literature is invariably frustrated in its attempts to fully verify a source for repeated sightings or to offer composite psychobiographies for the alien creatures who abduct humans. There's a sense of unresolved mystery about extraterrestrial phenomena which suggests that life-forms pertaining to parallel dimensions do not so easily intersect. Contact made by angels is usually subjectively inspirational, whereas that established by aliens is most often that of one species biologically curious about another. Reports of nasal implants, tissue-sample extractions and gynaecological examinations, abound in the literature of those who claim to have been abducted by aliens. If the poet sees himself as wrestling with the angel within the arena of psyche, then the combat is less physically pronounced. The contactee, however, often undergoes physical examination by his extraterrestrial examiners. 'Eternity is in love with the productions of Time,' Blake wrote – a theory which applies no less to art than it does to the overlap of angels or aliens with our lives.

If I look again at the experience which unites the mystic being visited by the angel, and the poet by the poem, I am inclined to call it an act of surrender. Both states of heightened awareness are achieved by a letting go of rational modes of interpreting consciousness and through being unconditionally open to inner discourse. We might call it letting the voice come through. Being swept off our feet. Crashing through barriers.

Is our first experience with love, first love, our initiation into the realization that angels exist? The sense of mystery investing the process or our surprise at being singled out, made singular by the other, is often the beginning of our feeling inspired. Reality is suddenly, dramatically and shape-liftingly altered by the adrenaline high we are experiencing. Everything appears charged and in the process of connecting with everything else. It feels that good when you're writing a poem. First love, if it is matched by youthful intensity, appears to have no correctable future. Neither partner wishes to entertain the idea of change. There is only now. The bite at the sunny-side of the peach. And what this love does so marvellously is to exclude reality. We dream of finding a habitable desert island and of sharing it with turtles and hear the soporific whoosh of surf conducting its dialogue with sand. But in order to realize the contents of love we have first to lose it. We acknowledge then that the nature of the angel is part black and part white. The kiss of love is also the kiss of death, in the way that the angel is both the messenger and the message. The angel is also there on that strange day when we walk back from the summer beach alone, swearing to die, swearing to never love or live again.

Sometimes, when I'm down, and in concourse with the blue angel, I listen to the singer Billie Holiday. There's a late song of hers, 'For Heaven's Sake', recorded in 1957, the year of her death, in which she sings: 'This pair of eyes/Can see a star/So paradise/Can't be so far.' In the simplest lyric form we have the highest aspiration. The lyricist has made the leap from seeing to knowing. The singer phrases this in a way that has us empathize with her vulnerability and her longing to know some completion through love. Holiday's inimitable intimacy of voice and her near-perfect timing make her one of the confessional voices that we take into our lives – and we do that because of the pact she makes with suffering. There's the sense of an angel being present in her behind-the-beat delivery. This woman, in her torch-singer's gown, has suffered so much that she speaks from the topos of broken hearts. That she can do so is due to the affirming angel. For pain to be balanced the artist must give it form, even if it does seem that the presiding angel has an ascensional wing pointing to the stars and a downturned counterpart signposting the void. Billie Holiday's creative legacy is that in attempting to heal her wounds she consoles our own. She's there to be played on rainy Sundays and on days when certain sorts of pain resurface in our lives. And for the space of listening we recreate the singer. Her image is reappraised: the white flower in her hair, the satin gown, the dark lipstick bow and the elbow-length gloves. We retrieve her from the underworld. She will help me remember my pain and, in revisiting it, to resituate that quality in my life.

When Orpheus visited the underworld to try to rescue Eurydice, he returned alone, but the value of the journey was in the experience. In a metaphor, he had evaluated the contents of psyche, he had penetrated to the interior and found himself sufficiently healed to make the return journey without the wife he had hoped to liberate. In the same manner, the torch singer cannot heal me but can have me realize ways in which I can heal myself. Isn't this what we mean by metaphorically dying into the song? By displaying his or her wounds the torch singer increases our potential to sensitize the archetypal figures of love and death. As a presence on stage Billie Holiday combined striking sensual beauty with the drug-ravaged dissociation of the junkie. She seemed always about to measure how far she could go and still continue to sing. The report back is always the celebration that the creative continues.

Why are some people creative? And I don't mean this in the psychotherapeutic sense in which life is a continuously creative process but more in the way of those who receive inspiration. Some are called, by which I mean to say that they have learnt to listen. Maurice Blanchot writes:

> The poet exists only poetically, as the possibility of the poem. And, in this sense, he only exists after it, though he stands uniquely before it. Inspiration is not the gift of the poem to someone existing already but the gift of existence to someone who does not yet exist.

Most artists express a certain degree of amazement at their creation. They are surprised by the outer form of what they had never before realized existed on an inner dimension. It's almost like being found out. People are shocked to know you had that within you. They often can't believe that the person they thought they knew was carrying such an act of subversive vision on the inside. The angel again. We often fail to see the invisible aspect of a person.

Time is an intensely private phenomenon. All of our lives we extract from it unconsciously and what we've gained from the process may not be evident until we come to challenge the perennial issues of love and death. In the process of forgetting we are preparing to remember. And what we remember is the true meaning of all those apparently blank days in which nothing appeared to happen. But wasn't there all the time a bird singing somewhere in the rain? And all the small detail of a world crowding into sight to be later reconnected with other associations, and this is the way that poems happen. It's often the synchronistic bridging of two apparently unrelated areas of experience that gives a poem charge. Analogical thinking centres itself on the image as the unit of poetic speech. Images are the building blocks out of which a poem is constructed. That Thursday afternoon, some time in childhood,

Raphael that the putto became transformed into the context of the Christian cherub, a dichotomized figure taken up by Michelangelo and Rubens but never fully disinherited from its ancient, Bacchic roots.

The equivalent of the putto today is to be found in inner space. We retrieve the image, which was after all a poet's and a painter's conception of an intermediary, and search for its counterpart in the external world. Poetry depends on this search for its continuity. The poet spends a lot of time looking, walking around and preparing for encounters with angels. There's a very real sense in which the poet goes outside to find the poem. He looks for it in unlikely places, and all the assembled integrants may suddenly take light, as he intersects with a beautiful face in the rush-hour crowds. That's what he was looking for: the stranger who he would never know but whose green eyes he would remember always as dancing-points along his nerves. And he might go out the next day and the one after and the one after that but he will never again meet that face. And so the longing for an angel begins and with it the directed stream of inspired poetry. Inspiration has been lit like a car firing on ignition. And who was that stranger? Somebody with a story, somebody surfacing above ground after their journey on the underground, somebody already on the way to a rendezvous, somebody about to buy a red Chanel nail polish or somebody about to choose a book which would change his or her life for ever. That person's story, no matter its personal or social biography, has become incorporated into angelology by a chance meeting in the late afternoon of a summer's day. Wasn't it such an off-chance moment that had Dante intersect with Beatrice, and out of that came the whole visionary architectonics of *The Divine Comedy*? Beatrice, too, may have been out looking for red nail lacquer. The schema behind great poems is sometimes one when we sat in the house alone excited by the prospect that our parents had gone out and listened to the rain come on and didn't yet know the meaning of what we were experiencing, was perhaps the beginnings of a poem. Years later that Thursday afternoon fills the visual and aural frames of a very different time. Something had been going on in the unconscious process for a long time, and a series of apparently unrelated events were the prompters to this weird marriage of sensory associations that we call the poem.

Telescoping into this space, James Hillman writes: 'A poem miniaturizes. It is like a computer chip or an optic fibre that carries many messages simultaneously. Such are metaphors.' And so it is a Monday at the end of the nineties and I am able to look into a window in 1964 and establish a connecting interface. Angels are a part of this in that they bring about universal simultaneity. When your communicating thought becomes a synchronistic happening you're in touch with the angel. You can think of them as fibre optics or any subtle means of telecommunication: telepathy or teleportation, for example. And you can be in touch in very simple ways by flights of active imagination. In the middle of the stressed, twitchy London afternoon you can imagine yourself sitting on a beach by the dark-blue Adriatic. You can make that quantum jump within seconds. We think ourselves where we want to be. In terms of consciousness the thinker alters the thought, like the percipient changes the perceived. In active imagination the unconscious plays the role of reality structurer: it recreates the universe. The poet, like the Vajrayana yogin who visualizes a deity into animated being, remembers the poem's topology detail by detail in the act of writing.

In the second of his *Duino Elegies* Rilke repeats his message: 'Every angel's terrible.' He addresses the angels as 'almost deadly birds of the soul' who he will, none the less, invoke by way of poetic celebration. Aware of our alienation from extraterrestrial beings, he writes: 'If the archangel, the dangerous one hidden behind stars, took a step down to meet us today: the mad beating of our heart would kill us. Who are you?'

This question which Rilke continually raises in his work, 'Who are you?', is pertinent to both the angel and the self. There can be no answer to this question for the directive is contained in the work itself. Rilke's relationship with the angel is one of attempting to place his trust in a force from which he feels disinherited. In the 'Seventh Elegy' he writes:

> Each slow turn of the world carries the disinherited,
> those to whom neither the past nor the future belongs.
> For even the immediate moment
> is far from mankind. This shouldn't disarm us,
> rather it should strengthen our resolve
> to keep on recognizing form . . .

By this Rilke implies that we should keep on recognizing the possibilities of the angel. The image of the naked, sensual putto, all blond curls and blue eyes, acting as an intercessor between humankind and the gods, a slightly more playfully pagan spirit than the Judaeo-Christian cherub, has been impressed on the Western imagination since the fourth century BC. The figure's elemental appeal, its pudgy, almost kitsch multifariousness and its apparent childlike activity all serve to invest it with a counterpointing sense of mystery. And often connected to the mysteries of fertility and regeneration, the putto makes libations or offers at the altar. He is often a cupidinous wine-bearer or a symbol on a funerary urn with an inverted torch. It's not until the work of Donatello, Bellini, Mantegna and, most significantly, of the accidental meeting with the prepared. Co-creativity on this level demands active and passive participants, poet and subject, both of whom are co-signifiers in the work. If there was a book depicting those who had inspired poems, the inspirers, wouldn't that comprise a visual geography of poetry, a meeting with inter-mediaries, no different from that of a universal angelology?

We all have our story the narrative of which is our own and everyone's in its continuous assimilation and projection of experi-ence – we're connected to it like a great river. And even when we sleep the story continues through the kinetic imagery of dream. The consciousness of the dreamer generates the space-time of the dream. And poetry is, of course, one expression of that story. It puts a clear eye on things. Poetic retrieval operates on the constant switch between conscious and unconscious levels, in the same way as angels are observed as emissaries crossing from one dimension to another. Poets see most clearly in the dark, by which I mean they are facilitated with the gift of seeing into the unconscious or the underworld. And in time, and with the experience of moving around in that world, comes the realization that the dark is also light. Angels inhabit both light and dark, and without close scrutiny of the shadow and without evaluating its symbolic mean-ing the poet lacks the adventurous sense of raiding the unknown which should be integral to the poetic journey. A poet is given the keys to the underworld and is called upon to unlock doors in the shadow domain of psyche. It is an error to write on the door with-out having first opened it and assessed the chimera on the other side. A poetry that seeks to avoid integration of the shadow will tell you nothing of angels. Apocalypse is really only individual change – it often means an inner cataclysm which occurs in some-body at a point which seems removed from time. The inner events may be contingent on breakdown, deep personal crisis or simply a shift within which is pronounced in dramatically archetypal terms by the unconscious. Apocalypse is a form of revelation. The revelation that begins whenever we cut through discursive thought and enter into the dynamically charged inner space in which we can be still and listen. It's there that the poem begins, and there that we connect with the universe. Everything enters that space and – remember revelation is about light – we apprehend what we were unable to see before. The poet does likewise: he establishes a metaphoric relationship between a set of responses which were previously unconnected and allows the reader to enter into that process too. What we experience in reading the poem is a revisioning of the universe. The imagery is the quantum mechanics of vision, for the poem establishes a microcosm of synchronous phenomena and allows us to participate in an area no longer structured by causality. The miraculous, the marvellous, the mythic, the archetypal, the Gestalt, all of these components are attracted by the poem's field. The poet works to accommodate apocalypse within our daily lives.

But finally, for all of us, it's in the huge experiences of love and death that we are most likely to encounter the angel. Somebody meets someone only later to discover that the angel comes to disappoint and finally disappear. He goes through a door at the end of the world, leaving a heart and a life in ruins. At the time there doesn't seem much left to retrieve, and perhaps then we may begin committing our feelings to poetry. The poem becomes the form in which we can elucidate emotional chaos. It also serves as a compensation for loss. Lovers write poetry, but the poet takes that process a stage further in that he universalizes the experience, he gives voice to a loss which is not only his own, it's everyone's. He celebrates universal absence.

Lovers are those who best understand death, for loving someone involves the acceptance that they will in time come to die. We suffer that. The hand which we are holding will, in Leonard Cohen's phrase, become 'rusted from the elbow to the finger'.

But we celebrate it, none the less, for all its qualities of affirmative beauty and trust. Those who write poetry are constantly in love with the other. The poet moves continuously towards a special date with the poem. It's incredibly exciting, making this adrenaline rush towards beauty and falling all over again into a stranger's arms. When I'm writing a poem I feel my excitement generated in every part of the universe. It's a fast neural buzz of energies. Somewhere else somebody's eating a bar of chocolate to simulate the feeling of being in love, and somebody's turning up to meet their date in a London park, while plane leaves are touching down like falling planets.

Let's go there one more time to meet love who is also called absence. You remember what? The heart-shaped ivy leaves trailing around the park-bench on which you're to wait. Big white clouds blow laterally across a mid-blue sky. Reality's really like a film set. You've brought a book of poetry in your pocket. This is a part of your life, but already while it's happening you're questioning whether this is really you. Don't we always doubt the lover will turn up, because of the mystery investing the other? We're always about to believe that we dreamt the person into being. It was a vision which can't possibly repeat itself – an illusion. You tell yourself those things and, as you do, you take up again with 'The Stranger Song', which kind of tells you everything:

> You tell him to come in, sit down, but something makes you turn around.
> The door is open. You can't close your shelter.
> You try the handle of the road. It opens. Do not be afraid.
> It's you, my love, you who are the stranger.

A HUNDRED YEARS OF DISAPPEARANCE

Count Eric Stenbock

WHAT is it, more than a century after his death, that has me take up with the extraordinary and perversely decadent figure of Count Eric Stenbock, who died at the age of thirty-five on 26 April 1895, the first day of Oscar Wilde's trial? Stenbock's own sexual propensities were similarly prosecutable should he have clashed with the law, but everything about Stenbock's existence evades proper biographical evaluation, just as his books have almost dematerialized and grown to be extreme bibliophilic rarities. Stenbock has become an extravagant fiction.

Stenbock's pronounced effeminacy, his self-destructive gravitation to excess of alcohol and drugs, his exhibitionistic dress, his cultivation of occult mystique, his inheritance of Estonian estates and the menagerie he kept all qualify him for a place in Huysmans' *A Rebours*, that *fin de siècle* compendium of pathological neuroses.

Stenbock's gifts as a poet were slight and his talents as a prose writer of Gothic vampire fiction confined to the single collection *Studies in Death, Romantic Tales*, which appeared in 1894, a year before his death. Stenbock's fascination with vampires, werewolves and the whole vocabulary of the night and oneiric underworld were not just derivations of his readings of Beckford, Poe and Le Fanu but a state of mind generated in part by drug abuse and in part by imaginative function. Stenbock seems to have manifested symptoms of pathological hysteria; his behaviour was paranoid, erratic, distraught, sometimes violent and often unpredictable. He interests me because he is an example of extreme states of mind and, while not being a novelist himself, he embodies the disturbed psychological characteristics which so preoccupied Wilde, Huysmans and Rachilde at the time. It might be said that Stenbock chose to become a fiction.

Who were the people who observed Stenbock in the street? He drew attention to himself, so how did they react? Transvestism seems to have been his mode of expression. The set of his bleached hair touched his shoulders, he wore bright silk shirts, oriental costumes, he painted his nails and used perfume and loaded himself down with jewellery, he took as his escort a life-sized doll, he was constantly stoned and, after his inheritance in 1885, ostentatiously wealthy. But he got around in London and not just privately, for he picked up one of his friends, Norman O'Neill, on the upstairs of a Piccadilly bus. It is evident that Stenbock took risks and, like Wilde, he undoubtedly 'feasted with panthers'. He lived at an angle to society and largely by night. He was seriously, rather than recreationally, addicted to opium, which he smoked with ritualized style, and his liver was shot through with spirits. He burnt himself out with the sort of dedicated self-destructive blaze of a Billie Holiday.

But there's more to Stenbock than an ideated degeneracy. Decadence wasn't the endemic mode of aesthetic expression in *fin de siècle* London and Paris that the accepted historical evaluation would have us believe. It was the exception cultivated by a number of distinct individuals, and its over-reach has come to colour most of the avant-garde cultural movements of the twentieth century. Stenbock's life draws attention to the separateness of the artist as outsider and the essential difficulties inherent in living out an alternative reality. He created and monitored a world in which he was the solitary occupant. He cultivated a life of altered states of consciousness, and at Kalk in Estonia, where he lived for two years subsequent to his inheritance, he kept a favourite monkey called Troscha who wore a scarlet shawl, had tortoises crawl about his sitting-room floor, fed his python on live rats and assembled a variety of toads, lizards and salamanders. Dressed in a green suit with an orange silk shirt, Stenbock lay in his peacock-blue bedroom smoking opium. His life can be viewed as a symbolic affectation or as a preparatory initiation to write the works he was unable to realize. Baudelaire wrote of the addict's fascination with free-floating autonomous imagery and of how this assumes precedence over the actual will to write. Poetry comes to be an invisible subtext to the smoker's passive monitoring of inner states.

When Stenbock does commit himself to the page, when he feels the necessity to externalize inner phenomena, then his writing impresses by the oddity of his perceptions. Inner and outer are never seamless, and it's the visible join which is the mark of creative tension. Take this passage from his fiction 'The True Story of a Vampire':

> Suddenly Gabriel burst into the room: a yellow butterfly was clinging to his hair. He was carrying in his arms a little squirrel. Of course he was bare-legged as usual. The stranger looked up at his approach; then I noticed his eyes. They were green; they seemed to dilate and grow larger. Gabriel stood stock-still, with a startled look, like that of a bird fascinated by a serpent.

The interchange here between imagination and direct natural description is unstrained. It's unlikely that Gabriel would have had a yellow butterfly in his hair, but we allow it, for the image of him carrying a squirrel is a vulnerable and natural one and in his prose Stenbock is well adjusted to the tension field created by the opposition of heightened reality to physical description.

Stenbock is Baudelairean in the sense that he has little purchase on the physical world and interprets the idea of it through sensory associations. His work was unrestrainedly homosexual within the allusive strictures of his age, and to a degree he was inhibited by lack of direct reference in that his emotional charge had to be modified if it was to meet with public expression. His poetry is scored by the singe-marks of someone fascinated by the concept of retributive punishment for his sexual propensities:

> I dreamed your soft warm limbs, my love,
> Burnt with hell's furious fire;
> And demons laughed, and said, this is
> The end of your desire.

In London, Stenbock lived at No. 11, Sloane Terrace, and later on at No. 21, Gloucester Walk, on the top of Campden Hill. It's unlikely that he saw much of London by day, though he did make the peripheral acquaintance of his decadent poet contemporaries and periodically gave money and refuge to the ruined artist Simeon Solomon. He lived by night like the character in Charles Aznavour's song 'Yesterday When I Was Young'. He was by nature solitary and knew he was burning a fast fuse to death. In the hope of modifying his self-annihilative momentum Stenbock surrounded himself with a world of contrived, ritualistic luxury. There is a story of how he would have dinner brought to him inside a closed coffin and of how he kept a red lamp burning between a bust of Shelley and one of the Buddha and how para-keets and macaws flew around his rooms. The atmospherics were stifling because of the incense and the opium exhalation, and Stenbock sat in front of a blazing fire distracted by his hookah.

Stenbock's reputation as an eccentric zoolatrist, an occultist and black magician, and as an aesthete who procured rent boys, is partly attributable to some of the obsessions expressed in *Studies of Death*. In his story 'The Other Side' he writes:

> There are things the top half like black cats, and the bottom part like men only their legs are all covered with close black hair, and they play on the bag-pipes, and when they come to the elevation then –. Amid the old crones there was lying on the hearth-rug, before the fire, a boy whose large lovely eyes dilated and whose limbs quivered in the very ecstasy of terror.

The centenary of Stenbock's death was in 1995. The inaccess-ability of his published books, and there appears to be at least one work, *Of Kings and Things*, of which there is no recordable trace, have accorded him the status of an almost invisible author to col-lectors of his period. Where have his books gone? We know that his family expressed displeasure at the homoerotic sentiments expressed in his first book *Love, Sleep and Dreams* and it is of course possible that after his death his estate saw existing copies of largely self-published books destroyed. Only the smallest number of copies have survived, a fact which has sustained the enigma of the Stenbock legend. We go in search not only of the man but of his absent works.

Arthur Symons has referred to Stenbock's Campden Hill address as 'a certain house, rather out of the way, one of a row of houses where several degenerates lived' and of Stenbock 'as one of the most inhuman beings I have ever encountered; inhuman and abnormal; a degenerate, who had I know not how many vices'. If Symons is correct, then Stenbock may have been living in a gay neighbourhood, but Symons is invariably self-consciously and melodramatically decadent, and in his 'A Study in the Fantastic' he helps accentuate the idea of Stenbock as social pariah. Do we conceive of Stenbock as the Quentin Crisp of his period, the *outré* cross-dresser who drew attention to himself by drag? And was Stenbock, who was so resolutely attached to the identity of being a poet, destroyed by the knowledge that he had misconceived his vocation and had only the externals of a creative dynamic? Perhaps he concerned himself too much with the occult, the grotesque and the bizarre and without the imaginative animation needed to transform his symbols into the new. His vampires are often metaphors for his sexual orientation. In his poem 'The Vampyre' he writes:

> In a serpent's coils entwine
> Thy supple and exquisite form.
> And drink from thy veins like wine
> Thy blood delicious and warm.

His writing manifests traits of Uranian necrophilia, and there is a willingness in Stenbock to shock, which is more confrontational in its sexual temerities than most of his contemporaries, excluding Wilde. His poppy-red wallpapers, the snake he trained to coil round his body, the thick Smyrna carpets, the perfumes with which he constantly scented his fingers, the roast peacock on which he dined, the whole overstrained neurology of the aesthetic addict were, in a way, a substitute for the lack of conviction in his poetry.

Stenbock died on 26 April 1895 at his mother's home, Withdeane Hall, near Brighton. Suffering from d.t.'s, he is said to have attacked a servant with a poker before collapsing with the haemorrhage which brought an end to his terminally cirrhotic condition.

He has survived a century in the imagination of those who celebrate the bizarre and the unconventional. Where would I find him on this cold, breezy April day in which I have chosen to bring him alive on the page? If he was up and out in the afternoon he would have had a taxi take him to Ted Baker in Floral Street. He would doubtless have liked their shirts. And his night? That is another story. A black car conveying him to the underworld and then back home to his exhaustive insomnia and the addict's slow discourse with the poppy.

POETRY, MADNESS AND
MASTURBATION

L ET me tell you a story. I have to chase through the decades to arrive there. If I incite a neuronal activation, a retrieval from the subliminal blue room in order to come back to you and re-present my findings, then the journey is similar to that taken in the course of writing a poem. It's the underworld myth. The hero returning not with his bride but with a simulacrum of her, his eyes big with the experience of loss but alive to the possibilities of creating out of the conflicting memories involved in his journey. There's a sort of post-coital, post-death glow which surrounds the writing of poetry.

When I was seven or eight I used to be taken to a park, a precinct in which my imagination learnt to come alive. I used to detach myself from my mother and watch dragonflies shimmer in low-flying trajectories across a pond. Their iridescent dazzle had me hypnotized. One afternoon when I was intently monitoring an almost close-up, translucent arrival resting like a jet fighter on a lily pad I saw the thing change, detail by detail, into what I would later come to know as humanoids, extraterrestrials and aliens. By which I mean the thing was metamorphosed into metaphor by my eye. It might have been a blueprint for a post-human species, the big wraparound eyes, the oval head, the body articulated into silver panels. I was seeing this while my mother sat near by on the grass, anxiously looking up at times to make sure that I hadn't slipped into the water. I can't say how long this cyberflash lasted; autonomous intersection with parallel dimensions isn't easily translatable into time. But I was neither invaded nor threatened by this transformative experience and, unnerving as it was, I made no initial protest about having slipped into missing time. I wanted to keep my vision secret. I knew instinctively that my mother didn't see such things and that I would be in trouble if I spoke of my findings. A dragonfly being metamorphosed into an android.

In retrospect, and after having spent most of my life inhabiting the inner world of image-arrivals or constellating psychic phenomena as it has found its way into my poetry and novels, I can evaluate the experience as a pre-initiation rite. My work has always been alive with mutants, androids, aliens, post-biological representatives of saucerian or extraterrestrial cultures and, almost alone among my poet contemporaries, I've made a poetry out of a sci-fi/futuristic/cyberspace ethos. I'm with the weird, the wild, the bizarre and the beautiful, the undercover agents who subvert stasis or convention.

My first arrival belonged to where? Inner or outer space, or a fusion of the two? Where do we locate visual or auditory hallucination? The image is pathologized when it seems to represent an inhibitory dysfunctional obsession. Poetry may differ from madness by virtue of its free-floating but dynamized imagery. It shows up at high speed like a car creating a parallax, a car burning towards an unlocatable destination, but I get the registration number down. If that crazy red speed-bug hurtles on a trajectory of over-reach into flame, I don't see it or care. What I get is immediate notation. I had to see it and it me. That's how bits of a poem arrive and break up into the work's contextual fiction. 'And me, I just don't care at all,' Lou Reed sings from the white core of his work. The clinicalized psychotic excludes reality for hallucination; he or she would go the whole way and be driven in the red sports car by the Virgin Mary wearing thigh boots and would probably never get off a journey which, to the poet, is a hot flash of implosive energy. Poetry incorporates reversible psychoses but never to the exclusion of reality. It doesn't stay long enough before it lets go. It's more that my madness comes from trying to arrest the temporal. Grabbing at the wind's tail and being left with a handful of sequins, like Judy Garland had just split her stage dress. The poet is closer to the magician in that he is in part protected by a rite. And poetry, at least the poetry I'm interested in, belongs more to the left-handed psychosexual magic advocated by the likes of Aleister Crowley, in which high attainments are achieved at the risk of a desacralized dynamic. Something like a raid on the angels occurs each time we set out on the poetic journey. I ask for the impossible and receive something of the fall-out. The messenger presents me with an image. Do I see it as a ruby, an emerald or a sapphire? And do I not punch it into the gates of the city or the city which is still to come? When we write with the imagination it is like catching stars. Their fires quickly cool, but a residue of the heat leaves a singe-mark on the page.

Occult poetry shouldn't be one which sets out to employ a specific, unnatural terminology in order to describe the suprasensual. I would prefer to think of it as a poetic state that assimilates non-specific weirdness. Esoteric poetry, *per se*, is too often flawed by an indeterminate diction. It's nerve endings are neutralized. All the crazy, up-ended jazz-syncopated rhythms inherent in accidentally psyching-in to parallel dimensions seem absent. It's more in the realm of psycho-magic practised by

Crowley that the explosive accident is likely to occur, the felicitous free radical on which the thing depends. The random arrival as it makes itself known through psychic visualization.

Where does sex come into this? The creative principle by its engagement with the subliminal erotic, or in magic directed towards sexual sublimation on a mental or physical plane, engages with polymorphous fantasies. The poet or the novelist positions his unconditionally compliant image as an interface to the equally authoritarian strictures applied by the magician. Both rely on the omnipotent subjugation of the partner or partners. Poetry is the ideal auto-erotic medium. From Baudelaire to the songs of Leonard Cohen, the erotic poet has learnt to transfer illicit desire into a received, celebratory mode of expression. I want you, or the idealization of you, so I fuck you in my head. The whole of de Sade's pornographic *œuvre* is supported by a matrix of pathologized sexual recrimination on a society which had him placed behind metal doors. Denied access to sexual partners, de Sade invented a world of mutilative atrocities and one in which he remained physically uncontaminated. He probably surprised himself by the escalating power he assumed in relation to his characters. His sodomitical propensities were realized by both sexes, but these where small pleasures compared to the inventory of sexual tortures he devised for the cast of his *120 Days of Sodom*. It should be remembered that de Sade is outside the work: he directs it like theatre; he is the voyeuristic control-freak who endlessly repositions the victims of his imagination. Introduced to the action he would probably have recoiled. He is the imagination pushing the cutting edge of psychological acceptance.

The sensual or the suprasensual, as it is worked by the imagination, is often the firing point to writing that pushes frontiers and which discovers the weightlessness of bodies in inner space.

Manipulation of the image means that the writer may be polarized to an opposite. He can discover on the line that the fat body to which he would normally have had an aversion becomes attractive through libidinous geometry. Leonard Cohen, one of the masters of modern erotica, and I'm thinking particularly of his novel *Beautiful Losers*, integrates Jewish mysticism into a collage of erotic and existential connotations in his enduringly profound songs. Here is one of his bizarre catalogues in the song 'Is This What You Wanted?':

> You were Marlon Brando
> I was Steve McQueen
> You were KY Jelly
> I was Vaseline
> You were the Father of Modern Medicine
> I was Mr Clean
> You were the Whore and the Beast of Babylon
> I was Rin Tin Tin
> And is this what you wanted
> to live in a house that is haunted
> by the ghost of you and me?

Cohen's usually heterosexual orientation becomes homoeroticized in the fantasy of his female partner turning into Marlon Brando and then into 'the Father of Modern Medicine'. Gender remains in a state of confusion again with his partner becoming 'the Whore and the Beast of Babylon', a transsexually apocalyptic figure and one that would probably not attract the singer in life. This is what I mean by the risks addressed by the erotic imagination. Gender and sexual preferences grow confused and may be reversed. We employ a certain sort of magic to reinvent a personal and universal mythology. Spontaneous lyricism, in which images are directed by psychic autonomy, often points up the integrants of bisexual or polysexual consciousness. We become somebody else in the volatilization of writing. And who is that intruder? Someone I carry around in my head all the time or a facet of personality channelled through a particular sequencing of the imagination? Or what about a walk-in, a psychic invader? I tend to think of the imagination as a series of high-frequency channels. I get one contact and another; static fuzzes in and warps the clear sound of the system and it's like signals bouncing off the microwave. Alien contact that I convert into a particular neurological code. The poem speaking for inner space. A poem represents a neurotransmitter which brings about a change in the whole system.

I want to return to the link between poetry and magic. Both occupations involve an absolute commitment to a left-handed tradition. Both go against the rationale involved in most politics and the extension of ideologies to the world of business emporia. Something of the continuous individuation was voiced by Aleister Crowley in a letter to an aspirant on 6 April 1923. Crowley writes:

> We conceive of you, and of every other conscious ego as stars. Each has its own orbit. The law of any star is therefore the equation of its movement. Having taken into account all the forces which act to determine its direction, there remains one vector and one vector only in which it will move. By analogy, the True Will of any man should be the expression of a single definite course of action, which is determined by its own characteristics and by the sum of the forces which act upon him. When I say 'Do what thou wilt' I mean that in order to live intelligently and harmoniously with yourself, you ought to discover what your True Will is by calculating the resultant of all your reactions with all other individuals

and circumstances, and having done so, apply yourself to do this will instead of allowing yourself to be distracted by the thousand petty fancies which constantly crop up. They are partial expressions of subordinate factors, and should be controlled and used to keep you to the main purpose of your life instead of hindering you and leading you astray.

Crowley's emphasis on freedom being attained through a singular pursuit of self-realization, whether it is through magic or the learning of the imagination, is one that ties in with the poetic quest towards ultimate vision or the insighting of an extra-temporal world. We all know of the opening of the third eye or the Eye of Shiva which, when activated, affords access to a substream of reality, a way of seeing in which the world of appearances is said to disappear. It is also the seat of mystical vision of extraterrestrial things. Kenneth Grant tells us:

> As such, anja is the Eye of the Light of Pure Consciousness, which in the Chinese magical tarot – the Y King – is symbolized by the trigram, L. This solar light is balanced by that of the moon in the next marma on the descending scale which is situated at the base of the brain, at the back of the head.

While the poet may not consciously work on the subtle energies needed to open the third eye, access may come about unconsciously and a metaverse of connecting signals come together in the brief metaphoric flash in which the image serves as the equivalent of its external symbol. This is called recreating the universe, seeing for the first time through the world of phenom-enal illusion. It's also something like a conscious and very deliberate raid on unconscious contents. Should I go too far or even further? Will I come to a level of insanity if I try to force doors in the underworld? There are chimeras behind some of them which, if they are provoked into day-vision rather than dream autonomy, may threaten one with an overview of madness. Fire may break out of a door, a man may step out with his head under his arm or a red dragon run like a horse through the corridor. And I may have to walk around with all that bite in my circuit, that overload on my nerves which could as easily blow. You could see this as a perverse ritual of self-divinization which ends in scorched wiring. Not that all underworld vision is inimical to sanity. Often the dark is a necessary means of counterbalancing light. We have to look, and look hard, at our subterranean findings. The bearable and the unbearable, the known and the unknown are all integrated into a central pattern.

My emphasis on Crowley as the archetypally poetic magician is not without pertinence to the connection between poetry and magic. Crowley would like to have been a great poet, but his verse is largely imitative, derivative of certain jaded aspects of late-nineteenth-century poetry and, in particular, mimetic of Swinburne. Crowley's poetry is expressed through magic and through his profound understanding of the symbols and accidental intrusions which occur in ritual magic. The sensationalism attached to Crowley, his conscious image of himself as the Great Beast 666, has been variously interpreted. That his extroversion was an auric disposition calculated to extract wealth from his patrons or to inveigle women to his cult is one aspect of his being. But the inner man, the magician, was serious beyond word. Crowley looked to establish on earth the cult of Love under Will, but the invocation of the True Will invariably resulted in its opposite. Crowley appeared as a demon to his devotees whenever the individual attempted contact with the 93 current over which he presided as the supreme initiator. If the initiate's aspiration in any way wavered in the course of confronting demonic experience then his moment of initiation had not arrived.

The magician, like the poet, is threatened by madness should he attempt to attain a level of consciousness for which he is unprepared. In Crowley's terms the Ipsissimus, or one who has attained 'his own very self', is seen as possessing 'no will in any direction and no consciousness of any kind involving duality'. The state demanded a total renunciation of illusion. Crowley, who took the oath of an Ipsissimus on 23 May 1921, describes only once, according to Kenneth Grant, something of the ordeal of his initiation which ran over the next three years and which in 1924 was to result in the death of his old life and the adoption of a new one. Referring to himself, Crowley writes:

In this last ordeal the earthly part of him was dissolved in Water; the Water was vaporized into Air; was rarefied utterly, until he was free to make the last effort, and to pass into the vast caverns of the Threshold which guards the Realm of Fire. Now, no human may come through these immensities. So in the Fire he was consumed wholly; as pure Spirit alone did he return, little by little, during the months that followed, into the body and mind that had perished in that Great Ordeal of which he can say no more than this: 'I died.'

Crowley is of course referring to the death of the ego and his rebirth through the transformative energies generated by the psyche. This form of metamorphic regeneration of the self is part of the magician's and the poet's means of making contact with the multidimensional, metasexual frequencies of higher consciousness. We go beyond ourselves to arrive. Crowley's attainments in magic are like the constituent components of visionary poetry. The journey taken by the poet is from image to image with all the high-speed neurological connections happening in between. If poets suffer from a syndrome known as temporal lobe dysfunction, which is the over-stimulation of right-hemispheric brain processes, then it would in part account for the direct conversion of sense associations into imaginative experience. That is, the striking of a match might instantly register as a aircraft diving in flames over a city. Or a dripping tap might be converted into the percussive roar of a waterfall smoking torrentially down a rock-face. Implosion is converted to explosion. Temporal lobe dysfunction is something I have known all of my life, and the extraordinary impacted sensation of audio-visual intrusion being converted into poetic experience is a part of my individual creative thrust. Right-hemispheric brain sensitivity will convert anything into anything. Neurologists attribute UFO abductee experiences to this source and the phenomenon of missing time surrounding the abduction. Cryptomnesia, insemination by extraterrestrials, amnesiac fugues, some of these parapsychological states are later resituated in memory through regression hypnosis, in the way that writing poetry can sometimes be likened to reactivating dream fragments through waking consciousness. When I'm writing I sometimes have the notion I'm training a video camera loaded with dream film from the back of my head to the page. The poem becomes, in the process, a kinetic assemblage, a construct of oneiric footage. My criterion for the success of a poem is that it should blow your mind. It should give you linguistic head in the process of reading it.

Head? I might get Anaïs Nin into the viewfinder here, the controversial supreme prose stylist. Nin, whose bigamous nature and imaginatively inventive erotica seem always to raise a storm of contempt and jealousy among her critics. Nin, who is at all times one of the most sensitive psychological prose-poets of the twentieth century, was also a prototypical female rebel whose erotic writings have formed a blueprint for almost all subsequent erotica that seeks to impress by its sensuality and imaginative plausibility. Nin took erotic writing away from pornographic expression; she articulated a medium that compelled by enticement and that counterbalanced explicit adventure with imaginative possibility. Nin is uninhibited because it is the nature of the imagination to go beyond safe contact into what I might call alien stations, or right brain colonies, where cell-clusters bump up with high-risk vision. Nin was an indefatigable translator of the minutiae of her subjective world into the rich possibilities of impacted prose. Nothing escapes the grab of her work. Her bite on the immediate is sensational. Her manner of using her material is Proustian in its diaristic qualitative evaluation of experience in relation to time. In the story 'The Hungarian Adventurer', from *Delta Of Venus*, Nin burns us with the dexterity with which she describes the Brazilian dancer, Anita, giving head to people in boxes at a Peruvian theatre. Nin appears to be invoking Lilith as her creative archetype.

There, on request, she knelt before a man, unbuttoned his pants, took his penis in her jewelled hands, and with a neatness of touch, an expertness, a subtlety few women had ever developed, sucked at it until he was satisfied. Her two hands were as active as her mouth. The titillation almost deprived each man of his senses. The elasticity of her hands; the variety of rhythms; the change from a hand grip of the entire penis to the lightest touch of the tip of it, from firm kneading of all the parts to the lightest teasing of the hair around it – all this by an exceptionally beautiful and voluptuous woman while the attention of the public was turned towards the stage. Seeing the penis go into her magnificent mouth between her flashing teeth, while her breasts heaved, gave men a pleasure for which they paid generously.

Everything here conforms to the rhythm of the imagination. There's a psychophysical fusion between the imagined and the real in Nin's descriptively experiential writing that affords it a sense of dead-on aliveness. We can imagine both author and subject contemplating each other in the evolution of the prose. Nin is discovering an extension of herself, like how the studied detail of a jewelled hand would enhance the aesthetic notion of fellatio. It's the image as it flashes into the writing eye; the detail as it enters the poem's magnetic orbit. Nin's spectacularity lies in her unshockability at the material she discovers in the act of writing. What the imagination locates in its deep fluent probe is often shocking to the writer. There's a moment in the process which demands a commitment to risk or a cancellation of the interfacing image. No matter how promiscuous Nin's personal life may have been, the enhancement of the erotic through her writing demanded high courage. What do you type in and what do you leave out? De Sade would have claimed there is no distinction between the two. Nin's sense of aesthetic stylization was nowhere more evident than in her insistence that she made herself up heavily with mascara and eye shadow and foundation before allowing the doctors to assist her in giving birth to a stillborn child in September 1934. Nin's biographer, Deirdre Bair, tells us: 'She disregarded any human element inherent in this birth, and from the beginning of the pregnancy seems to have considered it nothing more than an experience she could write about.' Bair considers Nin's actions to represent 'a portrait of monstrous egotism and selfishness, horrifying in its callous indifference'. For Nin, all experience was translated into writing. With Proust it was the same, and Robert Lowell used to continue writing poems while being stretchered towards an ambulance *en route* to the asylum. This method is to equate writing with alchemy. It's an ongoing process that hopes to arrive at eventual self-realization. And it's always there as a functional autonomy to those who are connected to its source. And what is it that has the poetic imagination endlessly convert one level of reality into another without there being any certainty as to a resolution to the process? Isn't one attempt at an answer the realization that inner reality is at its most valuable when it is heightened by conversion into imagery? Over the centuries the body of fiction which has arisen from the need to establish parallel dimensions of reality has grown to an intractable enormity. If all the books that were written were put together they would form a continent, a land mass we might call the outer geography of the imagination.

There is, without doubt, a dependency, one might even say a desperation, on the part of the inveterately compulsive writer. The inexhaustible generation of psyche through imagery leads the poet to recognize, in James Hillman's phrase, that 'the soul mediates the beauty of the invisible inner world to the world of outer forms'. Writing poetry is like attempting to unravel your veins, returning to the task again and again. There's no end to the mileage, the invisible becoming visible and the inconclusiveness of the process. Psyche, as an archetypal figure, is important here, for the last of her tasks involves the retrieval of a beauty not apparent to the senses. In Hillman's terms, she must inquire into the 'Box of Beauty' in the underworld, a beauty she knows would evaporate in the light and its contents dematerialize on exposure. And it's these contents and their sensory evaluation which are inseparable from the poet's vocation. Hillman tells us that her box contains 'the beauty of the knowledge of death and of the effects of death upon all other beauty that does not contain this knowledge'. Psyche must die in the underworld to realize truly the components of her ox of beauty, in the same way that Crowley underwent a metaphoric death in order to integrate the constituents of psychophysical initiation.

If I open the box I'm killed by the revelation; if I keep it closed I'm constantly fascinated by the mystery. The poet has to keep on imagining its contents. Is it a mixture of stardust, ashes, words in the form of jewels, dazzling metaphor and the unknowable mystery of death itself? Death with its purple eyes and surreal neurology. One of a million metaphoric guesses. Death with its . . . Death with its . . . Death with its . . . And how do I imagine Anaïs Nin dead, or more to the point what would her imagining of death have been? Her propensities for sensual luxury have me imagine her in the poetic halls of the dead, sitting at the top of a pyramid of silk cushions, crossing and recrossing her silk-stockinged legs while an unceasing queue of intended suitors mount the pyramid in continuous single file with the intention of winning her eye. And it's all an illusion.

For most people, their acknowledged contact with fantasy comes through libido. Sexual fantasies in waking or dream-states often involve autonomous risks that the person would never otherwise entertain. You imagine someone undressing or naked, you arrange them in various provocative positions that would appear to offer mutual pleasure and you may, through auto-eroticism, orchestrate orgasm through the visual fantasy. Poetry involves a similar autonomous manipulation of the image. It may activate the same level of pheromone stimulation as the rush of orgasmic release. The poet feels high after the poem's completion. He has also, perhaps, depathologized symptoms which may have been constellating around the obsessive images employed in the writing of the poem. Writing poetry may sometimes involve the expenditure of denuclearization of a pathological syndrome.

I want to know Nin from the reverse side of consciousness. Can I expect psychic fellatio from her contact? Will her black boa fall out of the sky on to my shoulders? There's a psychic extension to Lilith here, the demonic seductress or metamorphic succuba, who represents the essentially motherless forms of the feminine self. Nin was a tireless, nymphomaniacal seductress, who in embodying the instinctual side of femininity manifested a sexual-need orientation more often associated with the male stud. She laid men and, having asserted an irreversible hold over her lovers, then refused to commit herself to anyone in particular; rather, establishing a need in all of them that generated chaos in her personal life. Nin's restless promiscuity and her giving of herself to casual acquaintances has more in common with the gay sexual outlaw, in whose culture numbers are paradigmatic, than with a heterosexual ethos in which conception is the possible outcome of sex. In the Zohar, and in dreams recounted by women patients, Lilith is perceived as black and beautiful. Black, which is qualified as shadow, is also invested with the inner luminosity that Nin bought to her writing. The Zohar tells us: 'In the hour when the Matronit adorns herself and wishes to approach her husband, she says to her hosts: "I am black down below, and fair in my complexion above."' To confront Lilith in the mirror, and to recognize the destructive feminine within the individuated context of the self, is often a recurring dream or fantasy that women take into psychoanalysis. Nin appears to have been the embodiment of that confrontation, and in her short story 'Lilith', from *Delta Of Venus*, she powerfully portrays masculine fears of the primitively sensual in women. With acute psychological understanding, she accents the sexual incompatibility of a relationship in which there is masculine fear of female aggression. Nin writes:

> But Lilith's husband did not know the preludes to sensual desire, did not know any of the stimulants that certain jungle natures require, and so, instead of answering her as soon as he saw her hair grow electric, her face more vivid, her eyes like lightning, her body restless and jerky like a racehorse's, he retired behind this wall of objective understanding, this gentle teasing and acceptance of her, just as one watches an animal in the zoo and smiles at his antics, but is not drawn into his mood. It was this which left Lilith in a state of isolation – indeed, like a wild animal in an absolute desert.

It's hard to think of any other erotic writer who has so fully assimilated the complex associations of anima and animus that arise in sexual relationships.

I write poetry and fiction every day. I switch over from outer to inner, one frequency to the other as a natural form of discourse. My invocation, my connection is to Psyche, the underworld figure who retrieves imagery from her magic box for me and fists the hot contents into my hands. Every expression of consciousness has its requirements, an input that meets with an individual imprint, a resourcefulness which feeds the process of continuous individuation. Is poetry a pathology or a depathologizing instinct? Do I obsessively walk into a mad ward of imploded cells each day? Do I keep on opening the box to burn my fingers? Hillman writes: 'If Gods reach us through afflictions, then pathologizing makes them immanent, opening the psyche for them to enter; thus pathologizing is a way of moving from transcendental theology to immanent psychology.' I may see the invading disquiet surrounding my writing hours as a provocation of reversibly pathological symptoms. If poetry is viewed as an affliction, to take up Hillman's word, then the poet makes himself accessible to instruction through inviting madness. The god blows through consciousness like a sandstorm; the whiplash is the shock of realizing the visitation. Often when I'm writing, or in the spaces between writing, I listen to jazz and torch singers. No amount of poetic instruction could teach you as much about phrasing as Billie Holiday's voice. Always coming in behind the beat and inimitably personalizing the lyric through intonation, her sense of timing is near perfect. And in torch singing the diva's passionate devotion to unrequited love and the flamboyant gestural vocabulary that accompanies the singer's resignation to loss are not so far removed from the poet's desperate realization that only a part of his inner vision will be transmitted to the page. In writing, I am always moving away from myself; the experience goes one way and I go the other. I'm left as the external spectator, the voyeur to my inner world as it appears on the page. I almost wrote on the stage, for the poet's arena, rather like the singer's, is the conversion of inner pain into universally communicable experience. I'd like to change myself by what I write, but I only succeed in changing others. The line recedes as it expands, it becomes incorporated into its own distance, and I'm back to the red sports car travelling away towards an unknown destination. I'm both the driver and the spectator jumping up out of the grass to watch the car's manic trajectory burn towards the coast.

If, like Nin, Leonard Cohen's chief preoccupation is the sensually erotic, then he is also someone whose poetry embodies mystic discourse; a man whose natural expression in song is spiritual debate. Cohen's Jewish-Canadian roots, and his natural gravitation towards mythopoetic and allegorical narrative and his concerns with sex as the key to immanent mysteries, sometimes places him within reach of Crowley's Typhonic cult of the Beast and the Scarlet Woman. Cohen, too, would make inroads on 'the Whore and the Beast of Babylon'. Every sexual encounter about which he chooses to write offers the possibilities of initiation. For Cohen, poetry and sex share the same charge. The chemical change that the body undergoes during orgasm may be seen as instrumental in releasing the unconscious associations that contribute to creativity or, in Cohen's case, the writing of poetry. He can be hauntingly elusive in his conjuration of feminine mystery, as in the lyric 'Seems So Long Ago, Nancy' which he chooses to publish in prose paragraphs in his recent selection of poetry and songs, *Stranger Music*:

> It seems so long ago, Nancy was alone. Looking at the Late, Late Show through a semi-precious stone. In the House of Honesty her father was on trial. In the House of Mystery there was no one at all. There was no one at all.

As the compressed song narrative proceeds, so the promiscuous Nancy, who wears green stockings, kills herself with a .45 and takes up a place in the House of Mystery. And in death she becomes a fantasy for all the men who have known her: 'Many use her body. Many comb her hair.' Nancy is consigned to a passive Lilith role, a fantasy identified with auto-eroticism. At the end of the song, and in the middle of the night when the protagonist is lying awake, Cohen tells us that 'you hear her talking freely then. She's so happy that you've come.' The House of Mystery to which the dead Nancy has gone may also seem a place in which are stored a harem of masturbatory images. The disembodied feminine image belongs to Lilith's train. It's Lilith who vampirizes the sparks of semen left on the sheets after love. Lilith's metamorphic roles as seductress are portrayed again and again in Cohen's *œuvre*. In 'Death Of A Lady's Man' sexual perversity is amplified through the seductress saying: 'I'll make a space between my legs/I'll teach you solitude.' If union involves solitary pleasure then we know we have encountered an illusion or succubus. And in that space all women become the same: one image is interchangeable with another. Satisfaction is achieved only through an inverse form of pleasure; sensation is impacted and self-modulated in the way artistic vision falls short of any union between creator and subject other than an approximate or illusory one. I can't ever reach my vision so I keep on recreating facets of it on the page. I am trying all the time to see bits of my mind in the external world, incomplete printouts of nervous formulae. There's no end or beginning to autonomous imagery. If you have that particular sensibility, and you're hooked on it, the film never stops. Something of the paradox of circular creativity is expressed by Cohen in 'Avalanche', a song that ideally represents his mystic preoccupations:

> You who wish to conquer pain
> You must learn what makes me kind
> The crumbs of love that you offer me
> Are the crumbs I've left behind.

These lines are highly pertinent to the mystic source behind poetry and to the give and take within it: 'The crumbs of love that you offer me/Are the crumbs I've left behind.' The unresolved dilemma here is very much a part of the Lilith paradox. I return to an unresourcefulness which I must make resourceful. I must convert crumbs into gold. And the gold may be touched with a lick of the truth. 'Weeping I stared at gold, but could not drink,'

Rimbaud cries out in his *A Season in Hell,* suggesting that poetry is the ultimate confrontation with illusion. The poet holds the poem in his arms on the high road, but no one can see it. The process is one of the visible supporting the invisible. And again in Cohen's words: 'I am the one who loves changing from nothing to one.'

But in terms of poetry and magic, their interactive states are different branches of the neurological tree. The poet sits on one branch and dreams of tomorrow. Everything's possible. The big event may still happen. The imagination may become reality and the poet situate himself direct in the poem. And isn't the poem's tension field the equivalent of the circular nucleus of energy within which the magician operates? I'd like to cross over from perceiver to perceived, but it's the poem which interfaces this process. It's a unit of travel in terms of sighting inner reality. It's the quickest way to the stars.

HEROIC GESTURES

Scott Walker, Frank Sinatra, Marc Almond

SOMEWHERE in the history of torch singers, jazz singers, pop singers and crooners, if distinctions can be made in these always interchangeable categories of style, came a voice so inimitable in its heroic characteristics that it was immediately recognized as an ideal for singers.

The voice was, of course, Scott Walker's; his rich baritone thrust applying itself to tearjerker pop ballads that were made to sound like arias colouring a compressed wall of orchestral sound. Songs like 'Love Her', 'Make It Easy on Yourself', 'My Ship Is Coming In' and 'The Sun Ain't Gonna Shine Anymore', were singles that arrested a sixties generation of blue-hearted lovers, looking for the consolation afforded by moody songs. And it isn't that Scott was without predecessors. Elvis Presley, Roy Orbison and Gene Pitney, to name only three, had all endeavoured to infuse the ballad with sovereign meaning and to stagger the song's trajectory towards a vertical climactic axis.

But Pitney's yearning for heroics, evidenced in songs like 'Twenty-Four Hours from Tulsa', falls considerably short of the vocal expertise that Walker brings to a comparable ballad like 'Another Tear Falls'. If the comparison appears considerably to

Pitney's disadvantage, then it's at the expense of Walker's genius. Walker's beginnings, like his brooding literary concerns and his aspirations to transcend the narrower parameters of pop music, are of course mirrored in Marc Almond's initial success with the electro-pop duet Soft Cell. Both were singers constrained by a medium not only dependent on youth culture but also on the accessible hook of their material. And both had to earn commercial credibility before being allowed to experiment with their distinctive art forms within the study of singing.

In recollecting the initial premises of his friendship with Walker during the sixties, Jonathan King has pointed to Walker's intellectual passions at the time. 'One of his fascinations', King tells us, 'was Jean Genet and it was through discussing the character of this rather bizarre man that we found we had a lot in common.'

Genet, who is empathetically incorporated into the homo-erotic dynamic of Almond's creativity, finds his embodiment in Walker's psyche through shared aspects of inverted sainthood. Walker has consistently bypassed stardom in favour of pursuing artistic truth, in the way that Genet turned his back on the literary ethos of Paris and chose to situate his poetry in the underworld. Walker has progressively taken his work away from a commercial public and in the process has demythicized his pop status, choosing instead to pursue an anonymous and largely reclusive life. Almond has in some ways followed suit, though his periodic invasion of the pop charts has served to give him an altogether more public profile. An integral artist, he has, in order to secure recording contracts, found it necessary to revitalize his pop instincts from time to time in order to finance the more serious aspects of his work.

At the height of the Walker Brothers' success in 1965, Walker found himself listening predominantly to jazz singers and to the vocal stylists Frank Sinatra, Jack Jones and Tony Bennett. If the latter three are seen as great jazz-orientated pop singers, then it's more for their tonal colouring than their dramatic intentions. Sinatra described his own style as *bel canto* (literally, fine song) without making a point of it. It's a genre of singing that initially fascinated Walker, and his recording of the classic 'When Joanna Loved Me' on *Scott*, his first solo album, was succeeded by his mastery as an interpretative artist on *Scott Sings Songs from His TV Series* and the later *The Moviegoer* album. If Sinatra moved beyond jazz singing by completely democratizing beats and elongating rather than chopping phrases, so Walker applied a heroic romanticism to Sinatra's innovative technique. Sinatra said of his own method: 'You've got to get up and sing but still have enough down here to make your phrases much more understandable and elongated so that the entire thought of the song is there.'

Walker's attempts to push baritone romanticism to over-reach resulted in occasional vibrato, and for these reasons he was dispatched to the voice coach Freddie Winrose in Denmark Street. Both Walker and Almond manifest sporadic tremor in their singing voices, and both push a song to its limits and therefore risk failure. When the latter occurs, the resultant pitch is grandiose and Promethean, whether it's Walker chasing the speculative notes of 'Impossible Dream' or Almond pursuing the operatic undertones of 'She Took My Soul in Istanbul'. If this tradition of singing has always existed in France, and Charles Aznavour and Jacques Brel were both formative influences on the two singers under consideration here, then it remains an outsider's art within the study of British and American pop.

In his introduction to the Scott Walker compilation *Boy Child* (*The Best of 1967–70*), Almond credits his predecessor with having the supreme voice for the interpretation of the lonely song. 'His voice', Almond writes, 'has become a simile for all crooning deep tones and liquid vibrato' – qualities, he suggests, that make it an ideal instrument to engage with the themes of death and desire. Almond, who has recorded two of Walker's self-compos-itions, 'Big Louise' and 'The Plague', has also covered many of the Brel songs that Walker originally made available in English on his first three solo albums. In no way emulative of Walker's singular genius as a singer or the contracted, introverted sensibility behind the voice, Almond is still, in many ways, Walker's only successor. Central to their achievements is an incontrovertible belief in the poetic lyric as sanctioning voice. Their repertoires are narrower than Sinatra's was and more reliant on applying a histrionic inten-sity to obsessive narratives of loss and death. What Almond shares with Sinatra is his casting of himself as the romantic lead of most of the love songs he sings, a role that Walker, with his innate reti-cence, is more reluctant to assume. Almond subjectively agonizes, whereas Walker sounds more comfortable behind the screen of third-person heroics.

If Sinatra's egotism was what allowed him to portray himself in the roles of a desirous or defeated lover through his unfailing good taste in song, then it was his absolute seriousness as an artist that elevated him above his predecessors and contemporaries. It would be impossible ever again for a singer intending to make a durable art form out of the pop song not to cite Sinatra as the pro-totype of believable expression. Sinatra confides, and we are his ear. His taste for standards virtually defined the tenor of adult popular music.

I have used the example of Sinatra as a measure from which both Walker and Almond depart, and they do so by a dramatic torchiness of phrasing that, while it is sometimes flawed, is nevertheless a sublime attempt to project poetic emotion into song. And this, of course, has something partly to do with singing out of gender, a shift of axis that applies more to Almond than to Walker but is present in the work of both artists. Sinatra with his hats and his complacency about being very much a man, an image unfalteringly sustained by his life, is true to the archetype of the male singer. Like his influences, Bing Crosby, Louis Armstrong and Mel Tormé, Sinatra was beyond suspicion, and it's his absolute certainty in terms of gender role that contributes to the voice sitting so comfortably with the masculine ideal.

Walker's outstanding good looks, all high cheekbones and aesthetic sensitivity, were highlighted by the androgynous image made popular in the sixties. If his sexuality seemed ambiguous, then there were constant rumours of his being a nocturnal outlaw in search of the forbidden. Whatever Walker's sexual confusion, it's his state of deep inner disquiet that is communicated through his singing. What he brought to his huge sixties ballads, and which is absent from the work of Sinatra and his imitators, is a sense of using the contents of a song as a stage for unresolved anxiety. Sinatra comes to a song with the expectation of communicating emotional truths through elevated speech. In getting himself right in the early hours Sinatra does not doubt that he's got the listener's acceptance. The love songs written for him are largely about the understandable ups and downs in human relations. The lyrics eliminate the perversities, torments and inner crises that first Walker and then Almond were to implant into singing styles that seek redress from the angels. Sinatra's court of appeal is a bar, whereas Walker and Almond both address an etherealized dimension as much as they do a human level of conflict.

It would be easy to say that Walker expresses the new ideal and Sinatra the old – but Sinatra's method is the one still adopted by crooners. Almond, who struggles to maintain the heroic dimension in an age of horizontal singers, remains the solitary proponent of Walker's style. His failure either to confirm or deny publicly his putative gay sexuality has allowed him to take greater liberties in his choice of material, whether self-composed or chosen from the modern repertoire. He has, for instance, made a genuine, feeling song of Aznavour's 'What Makes a Man a Man', a number that Walker could have approached but has clearly avoided for reasons of discretion. Almond has had no reservations about singing from a woman's point of view, and the impassioned dynamic he injects into a song like 'A Woman's Story' sounds wholly authentic. The contrast with women singers like Nina Simone, who change the lyrics of a song to meet with gender conformity, is stark. Her disastrous attempt to switch the lyrics of the standard 'When I Was a Young Man' to 'When I Was a Young Girl' compares poorly with Almond's fluidity in adopting the feminine part in a song like 'The Heel'.

Walker approaches the issue with considerably more caution, preferring to narrate the story of the transsexual 'Big Louise' in the third person. The song's opening line, 'She stands all alone', situates the singer in his own isolated state. 'Big Louise', the story of a man who has become a woman, is the first pop song about a transsexual and was arguably the blueprint that inspired Almond's concerns with gender mutation in the subject matter of his lyrics. Walker and Almond differ from the Sinatra generation of singers in that the controversial nature of their material places it outside the limitations of easy listening. And here the question arises as to the nature of compromise in singing. Was Sinatra fulfilled by the relatively narrow lyric margins of his creative expression? Did the songbooks of Cole Porter, Rodgers and Hart, Irving Berlin and George and Ira Gershwin, to name but a few of the inspired songwriters at his disposal, really touch on the darker issues that were at work in his psyche? While singing was integral to Sinatra's life, I wonder whether there existed in the man a huge sense of frustration at the popularized material to which he gave that life.

Walker and Almond are romantics by reason of declaring their lives through their work. Unlike Sinatra, they have chosen to use the song as a medium of self-confession, an art facilitated by their abilities to write some of their own material. In Almond particularly, the 'I' that we have called the romantic lead of the song is naked in its vulnerability. It's a very different lead from the structured persona given to Sinatra by a songwriting team. Walker's self-regarding 'Always Coming Back to You' or Almond's 'I Who Never' are examples of self-composition that risk overexposing the artist but remain great by the temerity of the dare. Romanticism, whether it is in literature, art or music, invariably invites a savage form of critical hostility from its detractors who see the aggrandizement of the self as an unsuitable subject for artistic expression. The opposition between Dionysian and Apollonian approaches to creativity, the two poles of inspiration and reason, are brought into play here as the tension between subjective and objective styles of singing. Walker and Almond represent an imaginative affirmation of the individual as self-creator: the ongoing life is the source of the work. Sinatra and his imitators express a universal state of being, one which, while it pertains to the self, is neither self-consciously personal nor in any way dangerously confessional. A Sinatra record is likely to be assessed by the quality of the voice in relation to the suitability or unsuitability of the tunes recorded. An album by Walker or Almond permits the critic the additional arm of attacking the subject's personal life as it is reflected in the lyrics. And because of this both artists suffer for their work and experience a sense of self-defeat when it is unduly disparaged. Critics scent blood whenever they set to on romantic vulnerability.

Walker's arrival at heroic voice was linked to his love of Phil Spector's insurgent wall of sound, an effect he set out to recreate with the assistance of producers like Ivor Raymonde, Reg Guest and Wally Stott. The voice was situated in front of a compressed Wagnerian crescendo, all of it contained in barely three minutes of sound, the successful formula for a sixties pop song. The unorthodox juxtaposition of a baritone singer and a forty-piece orchestra combining to score monumental pop hits seemed to be as incongruous as it was short-lived. But after the Walker Brothers' demise in 1967 Walker employed the same musical tactics on his suite of innovative solo albums. Even if the material has grown more complex, the arrangements retain their sense of awesome magnitude. And the voice in its aspirations is always about to reach for the stars. Walker's interpretation of 'Angelica' on *Scott*, a song little discussed by his critics, is one of his finest vocal takes and exemplifies mastery of the romantic ballad. A song of broken-hearted longing in which the protagonist is made to reflect on his mistakes, he invokes the lost Angelica as though he is searching for her through the labyrinthine alleys of Venice. This is singing that is unsurpassed of its kind and one in which the resonant loneliness of the voice creates a new way of addressing unrequited love. Walker's natural method is to foreground romanticism and to use it as the unashamed principle on which the song is structured. For Sinatra, the romance within a song is coloured by his use of nuance and inflection, and it is almost never the dominant theme he takes up to bring the song home. Walker and Almond are the first operatic pop singers, in that within their respective limitations of voice they employ the coloratura of the greater medium. Walker's total commitment of voice in songs like 'Montague Terrace in Blue', 'The Amorous Humphrey Plugg' and 'My Death' finds its only parallel in Almond's bravura apparent on numbers like 'You Have', 'The Stars We Are', 'The Slave' and 'A Man'. At his most successful Almond continues to vitalize a medium begun by the older singer, while elsewhere he is torchier than Walker and more camply theatrical in his delivery.

What is most valuable in creative expression is usually uncategorizable and belongs to the edge. There have been no shortage of good singers influenced by Sinatra, and among them we should include Johnny Mathis and Matt Monro, but male torch singers are a rare breed, with Almond remaining the only British exponent of an essentially female art form. The argument for Walker being Almond's male torch predecessor rests on the strength of Walker's first three solo albums, with their Frenchified influences and cathartically charged emotional singing. But tenderness and compassion, too, are a part of this register. Walker's sympathies usually remain with the woman's broken heart in the song. His sensitive character studies of women in songs such as 'Mrs Murphy', 'Rosemary', 'Big Louise' and 'Genevieve' and the compassionate way in which he sympathizes with how women respond to loss are the psychological components that link him to torch song. He doesn't, like Almond, sing from a woman's point of view, but his empathy with ways in which women suffer contributed to the early image of Walker's ambivalent sexuality.

Sinatra's career may be seen as an attempt to preserve the music of the great modern songwriters, a task that aided by Nelson Riddle's subtle arrangements he has succeeded in doing. In his fine study of contemporary singers, *Jazz Singing*, Will Friedwald expresses a sentiment about the intended durability of

Sinatra's work which seems to pinpoint the singer's intentions. Friedwald writes: 'More important than even his conception and perfection of the swingin', lover style, the dominant idiom of non-rock pop singing since the fifties, Sinatra sang and thought in long form, deliberately seeking to create music that would outlive him.'

The almost conscious acceptance that his voice will be recognized by posterity is very much part of the assumed Sinatra arrogance and the way he sits so well with song. And, if you can only be imitated and not bettered, then an art form may become too fixed and, arguably, the ability to have put some of the chaos of his life experience into words would have provided more tension in Sinatra's *œuvre*.

Neither Walker nor Almond are pretenders to *bel canto* and, if anything, the former has worked to deconstruct the natural facility he possessed for this particular expression of song. Walker professed himself to be bored with his facile interpretative successes like 'Joanna' and 'The Lights of Cincinnati' and was far more at ease pushing Jacques Brel's dissolute character-sketch 'Jackie' into the charts on the tail of its having been banned from radio play because of its offensive lyrics. Walker and Almond have both been the subjects of media censorship, in the same way that Baudelaire and Flaubert were both prosecuted by obscenity courts for writing that was considered scandalous in *The Flowers of Evil* and *Madame Bovary*. Some of Almond's most richly inventive singles, songs like 'Ruby Red' and 'Mother Fist', have fallen prey to a censorship unable to separate poetic lyricism from its degrading counterpart, prosaic pornography. It would be inconceivable to think of Sinatra risking lyrics that were not in accepted good taste.

I imagine that both Walker and Almond would argue that any expression of inner or self-truth is likely to risk sounding controversial. Both have their origins in a sixties and seventies generation of pop musicians who used music as a subversive weapon to undermine the then pervading socio-sexual ethos. Taboos were broken by sixties pop music, and something of that challenging thrust to tradition is incorporated into the angular dynamic of these two singers. Both could have become the cabaret artists or crooners that the Sinatra generation saw as their legitimate milieu, but neither has pursued the possibility as a commercial option. Instead, each has sought to diversify, to live within a metamorphic world of musical changes. Almond oscillates between devotion to the torch ballad and affiliation to dance music, while the hermeticism of Walker's last two albums suggests that he is moving more towards the experimentation of modern classical musicians and has come to use his voice as a neutral instrument rather than as a declarative vehicle of romanticism.

Almond's unusual role in male singing has something of the extraordinary about it, which touches on aspects of Shirley Bassey's dominance among female torch singers. His camp theatricality and unashamed willingness to portray vulnerability and hurt in the male finds a parallel in Bassey's use of song to compensate for the vicissitudes of love. But Almond has not, to date, allowed himself to become as committed to one genre as Bassey, though he will probably settle in to his role as he grows older.

Pop singers of Walker's and Almond's category have a difficult time justifying themselves commercially to a corporate record industry. They are cult artists who lack mainstream appeal. Progressively marginalized, they have each negotiated ways of survival: Walker through the legendary status of his past and Almond by seeking opportunist hit singles to allow for fan-base-only albums. And, though still revered by rock reviewers and upheld by an older generation who have remained loyal to him from the start of his career, Walker has distanced himself from his pop roots by cultivating obscurity and basing his melodies on the sort of technological disarrangements that have become an integral aesthetic to Brian Eno. Walker's use of scrambled lyrics and deconstructed compositions has something in common with the innovative aspects of David Bowie's Berlin period in the seventies and with the latter's return to an Eno-collaborative deconstructionism on *Outside* (1996). Walker's musical career describes a trajectory from romanticism to postmodernism.

In the concert programme for his 1992 Royal Albert Hall appearance Almond is described as a 'traditional singer', someone at home with the ballad form but equally capable of performing torch songs to electronic music. In this respect his chosen polarities have never changed and he is still as likely to come up with a slab of gay disco arrangement as he is a string-orchestrated ballad. If Walker has for personal reasons performed a disappearing act, enforcing his natural propensities for reclusiveness with a twenty-year absence from the stage, then Almond, if he is to retain a place in pop, is forced to foreground himself in the public consciousness. In that way he remains an undefeated romantic, even if the bridge that supports him from the fuming abyss roaring below is a precariously thin one. Almond feels the necessity to challenge the pop charts but, like Walker, he may at some stage concede on that issue and elect instead to record material more concentratedly in harmony with the poetic side of his sensibility.

Sinatra, rather than diversify into mediocre eclecticism, remained true to swing, the music form that best suited his voice. He was a realist as opposed to a romantic, and part of his credibility as a singer is that he appeared to be talking directly to you. Whatever the various moods explored on albums as different as *Songs for Young Lovers, In the Wee Small Hours* or *Only the Lonely,* all from the fifties period of Sinatra's career, the homogenous feel of the singing, whether it is wistfully romantic or tending towards *film noir* resignation, is always one of plausibility. Nobody is going to doubt what he related or that he was a feeling-singer given to grounding the emotion in his songs. The sense of disillusionment or world-weariness that he imparted to his tone was all part of Sinatra's image of somebody for whom love no longer held any secrets. He had seen through it all. Affairs create the same cyclical consortium of problems and Sinatra articulated most of the joys, doubts, uncertainties, pleasures and pains of heterosexual relationships in the course of more than half a century of singing.

Almond's emotional trajectory in song entails considerably greater risk. He is often perceived as a gay artist who may take homosexual love as his theme and is therefore someone unlikely to conform to a Las Vegas repertoire. His unconventionality is his strength, but it entails the necessary sacrifice of large-scale popularity.

Walker, too, in his reaction to *bel canto* has gone for limited popularity in favour of maximum integrity. Admirers of the voice as something distinct from the man tend to see Walker's career as one of wasted opportunities in which personal neuroses have prevailed over a remarkable talent. Appearing to have become ordained to increasingly longer periods of silence, Walker has grown to represent speculative potential rather than realized projects. The great resonance of the voice is kept on imperturbable hold. What we largely hear are his recordings from the past time-jumped into the present. His voice has alerted the sixties, seventies, eighties and nineties to its original romantic structure without appearing to belong to any of them. Over a long period of time the recorded voice grows to sound disembodied or even posthumous. 'Make It Easy on Yourself' is likely to catch you out somewhere in public, its displacement in time almost overwhelming as Walker's baritone emphasis forces the song to improbable reaches. And for those of us who were aware of the song's original release, its survival as something always immediate to the listener provokes a whole series of memory associations concerned with a past compressed into the time duration of the song.

Whatever the merits and defects of his mode of singing Sinatra stayed on top of the musical world and held to that pyramidal summit, no matter the arrivals and departures of pop acts as big as Elvis Presley, the Beatles and the Rolling Stones. Uncontested in his own generic mode of singing, Sinatra's voice imprint is possibly the most indelible of the last half-century. Without an heir to his title, his legacy lies in the continuity of his vast recorded archives. Late-night reflections on the flipside of our lives, and the rainy blue aspects of how we perceive love, will always make Sinatra's music indispensable. He and Billie Holiday will continue to companion our solitude on those Sundays when we stand at a high window overlooking the city and attempt to correlate the emptiness of the thin blue sky with the vacuum we feel in our lives.

Like books, records go out of print, disappear for however long it takes a reputation to be critically reappraised and then resurface. Walker's solo output lay dormant for twenty years before Fontana rereleased the major albums on CD in 1992. In this respect his silence had been absolute. There was no new work and the legendary albums from his past were unavailable. But somehow the achievement was never forgotten, and I suspect that both Walker and Almond will always occupy a place in the history of romantic pop singing. Their work exists independently of chart popularity and has come to describe a cultural aesthetic more readily identifiable with French *chanson* and with the enduring qualities of the best torch, jazz and pop singers.

If Walker's voice initially created a role for the romantic hero, then it's in this vocal cast that he's remembered. The modification of that style to suit his harrowingly intense and lyrically abstruse later albums is a creative transformation known to a smaller cult. In the collective memory he will always be situated within the space of the big ballad, no matter that he has disowned his allegiance to this dramatic form. He is the progenitor of a way of singing that, while it clearly separates itself from the style made popular by Sinatra, is none the less within the parameters defined by traditional singing. Almond's work has modified the position again. By deliberately testing romanticism on the pop charts through ballad and dance expressions, he has chosen to subvert the latter medium's basic simplicity by contrasting it with finely executed vocals. He has also given us superbly empathetic renditions of songs from the major writers of French *chanson*: Jacques Brel, Leo Ferré and Charles Aznavour. The two albums *Jacques* (1989) and *Absinthe* (1993) find Almond developing a sensitive tenor's range and an ability to use short and extended notes on diverse and complex material.

It seems unlikely that Walker will reaccommodate the romantic idiom to his future style of singing. He is like someone who has set fire to a house and walked away from the charred ruins to embrace a new anonymous identity. Almond has lit a torch from the embers and his cult assemble whenever he pulls the brand from his heart and exposes its heady flame. The romantic agony was how Mario Paz termed the dynamic behind those writers who dedicated themselves to a self-destructive inner truth. Walker either didn't want it or was unable to sustain his quest for the romantic ideal. Almond still dances among the flames, willing again to commit himself to the heroic gesture. 'Remember the hero returns' Rilke wrote in the first of his *Duino Elegies*, and we who listen to the voice await Walker's next musical incarnation.

Reflections

'Soul Inside'

MARC Almond's peculiarly idiosyncratic cocktail of archetypal torch singer working within the dynamic of pop has, for nearly twenty years, comprised an act so individually audacious, so uncategorizably focused in its determined energies and so heart-felt in emotional context that we have all come to feel the 'soul inside' his vocal register.

The resurrection of the song 'Soul Inside' to his repertoire for concerts at the Shepherd's Bush Empire on 14 and 15 December 1995 reaffirmed the 'wild celebration' of that song, with its tenacious, impassioned cry to hold on regardless of the maelstrom of psychic debris which builds up on the inside. Written in 1983, an emotionally distraught time in his life, and issued first as a single then as a track on the album *The Last Night in Sodom*, 'Soul Inside' speaks from an indigo bruise and instates a corresponding empathy in the listener to search out old scars and reopen them in the course of listening to the song. It's like psychic surgery. It's all done by voice; kinetic lasers operating on the inside.

John Keats considered that 'soul making' was the criterion which justified individual destiny. We build within in order to give voice to personalized experience. Our souls accumulate psychopathologies, and the pathologized elements become the vocabulary of subjective discourse, the index by which we alert ourselves to who we are. The depression, the elation, the repression, the things done to excess or overkill.

Soho, to those who know it, is a village, an enclave of interconnecting streets and alleys, and it's impossible to divorce this specific topography from much of Almond's lyric impulse, in particular during the period when he wrote 'Soul Inside'. And Soho is there again in 'Adored and Explored' in its reference to 'wild, wild child of the London night' but is more acutely there to the foreground in Almond's song-writing when he was a Soho resident living opposite Madame JoJo's in Brewer Street.

'The wind in my hair/And the black in my eyes/I was holding back tears/As I reeled with surprise,' the song begins, the voice coloured by Gary Barnacle's offbeat sax, its oblique trajectory complementing the narrative's immediate up-ending of gender. It's a man who is endorsing the romantic conception of 'The wind in my hair/And the black in my eyes', not a chanteuse mussing her lipstick in a French movie. It's impossible to think of any other male singer who would have had the temerity to make this confessional overture at the time and even more inconceivable now when mainstream pop has been reduced to quotidian expression.

Confronting madness, touching on the peripheries of reversible psychosis, pushing the frontiers of nervous breakdown, these are all pathologies symptomatically concomitant with risking everything through creative output. Almond's song under consideration here is precisely about such things: a hyped-up, pilled-up, traumatized grab at everything, as though his leather-gloved hands pulled at a collapsing ship's rail in mid-Atlantic. Is the protagonist forcing the rail or holding on to it? 'And the beat of my heart/Marks the passing of time/And I just want to scream to the sky' is the desperate predicament voiced with the soul feeling of someone confused about whether singing is the poison or the cure. And once you're conscious that every heartbeat is a division of linear time, an incremental accretion that erodes mortality, then life adopts the pace of manic hysteria. The subject is understandably 'waving good-bye/To control of my mind'. Too much pressure, too many margaritas, fan encampments on the doorstep, the whole confusing, belligerent pace of Soho leaking into the cells, and so the song has its infrastructural centre in the contention between private and public lives. At the time Almond described himself as a 'wailing, over-dramatic self-destructivist with diva tendencies', and 'Soul Inside' is driven by this fusion of volatile characteristics. One could imagine the number performed in a flamenco style, but its brassy up-tempo keyboard lurch and understated sax give it the frisson and implosive oddity which make it a song which carries you to the end. The end is retrievable breakdown and the assassination of Soft Cell's career and, in the video accompanying the single, Almond smashes his tokenistic pop trophies while being blown away by the assault of a violent wind. He sings the song against the grain, straining against the storm, forcing the lyric open in unpropitious conditions. The voice comes alive like a red desert flower, all the more generous for the prevailingly hostile climate. A red flower triumphing over grit and stone. And aren't there leather vultures creaking near by in the indomitable blue air, as there are leather boys lining the Old Compton Street bars?

On its release 'Soul Inside' charted at No. 16 and suggested yet another experimental tangent for Almond to pursue in his multi-faceted eclecticism, but Soft Cell's flirtation with more outright pop was hardly to survive the release of that single.

The soul is the repository of archetypal realities. It's the intrapsychic arena in which myths are perpetuated and individualized. Bulls stampede its boundaries and menacing beasts filter into the unconscious. Creativity, and voice is a measure of that force, is about imposing order on chaos. Almond gives a controlling shape to incipient madness in 'Soul Inside', his voice gets above the inner debris for the blazing three minutes which constitute an eternity in the compressed experience of listening. Time expands and seems without limits in the act of abandoning oneself to music. It is to perpetuate this illusion that singers dress for the stage, even if their slot is only one that lasts a few minutes. We often come back to a song in the hope that it will redeem us from the passing of time.

What's the difference between 'Soul Inside' as it was delivered in 1983 and the same song given a vitally passionate rendition in 1995? The distinction of a live performance is, of course, the singer's personal biography and the deepened experience he uses to enhance phrasing, but on record, in the course of listening to it, the song is fixed. The voice can never age. It belongs always to the present tense. In performance the song adopts a historic context and we are conscious that, after a gap of twelve years, its singer has changed and is rereading the material according to experience gained. And even though you can't see a soul you hear its contents in Almond's phrasing. The emotions take on sonic intensification.

Poetry is my magic. I often tell people that I catch images like falling stars in my hands. But it's a different form of listening, involving silence. Singing is about externalizing that process through audible breath. 'Soul Inside' is the best-sung evocation of madness that I know, a strident assertion of reckless inner portent transformed through urgency into the stability of form. You can't hold the song. You reach for it like grabbing at the wind's tail. You can listen to it at high speed in a car racing towards the coast or in a black armchair which appears to lift mid-song, adopt its own flight path out of the building, circle the nearby heath and return you three minutes later to your familiar room.

'L'Esqualita'

How do you tell a woman's bottom from a man's? It's usually a matter of gluteal cells. Women have 40,000 million cells contributing to their provocative curvature, and men possess half that number unless, as when a man changes gender, they undergo cosmetic surgery. Drag is the *outré* personification of the opposite gender, a man's adoption of female characteristics and the exaggerated overemphasis he places on that simulated femininity.

You could argue that 'L'Esqualita' is not only one of Marc Almond's best songs but one of the finest evocations of drag in the milieu of torch music. Right from the first note the pronounced ambiguity of gender becomes the song's epiphanic theme: 'Oh, I could believe/That she's a real diva/She tugs at the reins/Of a hundred Chihuahuas', the whole boaed, sequinned, physiognomically transmogrified gender-mutant playing up to the spotlight to deliver a ballad. And who do men who impersonate women imagine themselves to be? Ava Gardner, Rita Heyworth, Jean Harlow, Marlene Dietrich, Brigitte Bardot, Marilyn Monroe? That 'ten-minute ballad of despair and blood' has no past or future for the performer. The concentrated present, the magnified point of visual and aural focus which the singer becomes, allows him or her to disinherit their natural birth and to exist only within the time span of the stage. Up there a man is licensed to be a woman, or a woman a man, all historicized personal biography is eliminated, and so a star is born.

Of course, in 'L'Esqualita' Almond is both the singer and the singer in the song, as though a Cocteau trick of mirrors allowed a single image to adopt a dual life. It is Almond who is characteristically the vocal source of despairing ballads, heart-in-the-throat invocations to unrequited love and Thanatos, the youthful god of death. Lyric escapes the singer's throat like mythic fire. Breath retrieves the continuity of collective emotions.

In the song the drag-artist 'Sings of her sequins/With tears and with traumas', not as a real woman but as a man suffering for the imagined perfect woman within him. The pain is even more real for the excruciating gender paradox: 'And OK so it's ham/But she means every word.' Listening to a song is what? A form of empathetic osmosis? A distraction? An attempt to resituate oneself in the real world? An attempt to be transposed to the singer's world, that inviolable inner sanctum which exists inside the song.

'L'Esqualita' is pop cabaret. Gary Barnacle's sleazy, showtime sax hints at drag striptease, as well as the decadent sexual politics of 'a fistful of love with Raoul Kowalski', as though fisting were the natural connotations to his being 'only a slob of a Corsican junkie'.

What I love about the song, and I want to get right in there, is the idea of the drag-singer spending 'the rent on a new dress', that sort of impulsive, reckless irresponsibility which wants to burn up in the moment irrespective of the bills or the future. Wardrobing the instant is a part of drag, the need always to appear as a finished woman, someone who excels by way of feminine ostentation.

Running out into the street, a scene in the taxi, dresses spilled across the bed, the whole crazy extravagance of living out of gender – the song gets all this squarely into orbit.

The alphabet of drag is rhinestones, an artificial-paste medium, a fake currency which rains into blazes under the spotlight. Rhinestones confirm the illusion of glamour. So do sequins. 'Diamonds are for ever' is the leitmotif of another song, but they are the prerogative of a woman's beauty and not the vocabulary of drag. Conchita Piqueur is consigned to being a 'Carmen in cling film' as she assimilates the applause. No amount of restructuring, collagen or liposuction can make inroads into her sexual dilemma. A woman in a man's body becomes a man in a woman's body. There is no way of rectifying the issue.

When Almond detaches from the song and addresses his involvement in the first person singular, it is with ironic contempt for the crowding pressures in his life as a pop star: 'I'm so sick in my spare time/Humouring thugs/We could go out to dinner/But we're always on drugs.' This repeated refrain is delivered with a contemptuous sneer, as though Almond has come to this 8th Avenue Spanish Puerto Rican drag club called 'L'Esqualita' to show the side of himself which not only the tabloids ridicule but which is fraught on the inside with hassling parasites. The price for being a voice of creative dissent is one of attracting the curious who, even though they are sympathetic, simply wouldn't dare to go public in support of unorthodox sentiments. And you notice how no singer has ever dared to cover 'L'Esqualita', despite its anarchic, cutting-edge sexual politics. You could imagine that drag was invented for this song and not the other way round. The song comes straight out of the vocabulary of his sympathies for transvestites and transsexuals.

If there's one thing to be feared in life it's the mediocratized collective, by which I mean the straight man's justification that he's straight. The song 'L'Esqualita' celebrates a world in which everyone is their opposite and an ethos in which recreated gender is cause to celebrate the difference. 'Chi Chi at the bar/Dressed à l'Esqualita/Talks of Johns and of Joans/And tomorrow's rhinestones' is observed reversing society's customary ridicule of drag and is instead the object of applause, a glamour apotheosis within her own milieu. And when we wish to recreate her she's there through the instructions of voice, in the way that singing is a form of narrated visualization, a resurrection of words which no longer just sit on the page but take on the phrasing and intonation of dynamized breath. Conchita Piqueur will always come alive to the listener, now or whenever. The voice raises her by breath. Singing is a form of instant retrieval, a way of bringing intangible, oral characterization alive.

'L'Esqualita' hasn't ever been a regular live fixture in Almond's repertoire. The song came up at Soft Cell's two farewell concerts at the Hammersmith Palais in January 1984, then dipped into obscurity until he revived it for a number of acoustic concerts in 1991 – notably at the Passion Kirche in Berlin and for a series of shows in Japan in the summer of the same year. Enrico Tomasso would have afforded the song instrumental flourish and colour in his association with Almond in the mid-eighties, but the chance was dropped. The song awaits restoration in the future context of his live performances.

Let's go back into the bar. 'With one hand to the bosom/Paid for by the ballad', a wonderfully elliptically compressed way of referring to breast implants, the singer is none the less true in her projected emotions: 'And somewhere in there is a deep love for love.' The latter sentiment gives rise to the compassion on which the song hangs; the line is repeated for emphasis and Almond's voice feels for the authentication of heart in the genuinely tragic balladeer. This is of course where subjective empathy enters into lyric writing, for it is the feeling – expression – in Almond's heart which lifts every line he sings to epic proportions. I like to listen to this song before I go out to Soho, particularly on a rainy day, immersed in the poem or novel I am writing, sitting for an hour at Maison Bertaux, and then collecting memories in the maze of alleys leading off Wardour Street. I have seen William Blake reading out of a gold book in Broadwick Street and a rainbow open a pink rose over Meard Court. And 'L'Esqualita'. It's *the* song if you're in gender mutation, and the voice behind it is the consummate one if you love women who are men and men who are women.

ENDGAMING

Scott Walker's Tilt

for John Robinson

WHAT do legends do in their periods of being away? I mean, did Lautréamont, the author of *Maldoror*, really die on 24 November 1870 in a modest hotel, 7, Faubourg-Montmartre? Was it really the 23-year-old body of a mad genius, the prototypical *poète maudit*, who was found dead of unspecified causes on that hotel bed? Or was the real Lautréamont, or Isidore Ducasse, drinking in a bar in another quarter of the city, glad of the trick he had played on posterity and about to take up an anonymous life as a drag artist? We'll never know. History is a continuous fiction and its inventions afford us access points to time. *Maldoror* happened in 1868 as an event in Lautréamont's biology. *Tilt* occurred in 1996 after Scott Walker's having been absent from recording for a period of thirteen years. Walker had been presumed dead, mad or simply dysfunctional by the few who speculated on the reasons behind his absence. An absence that involved absolute silence.

If Lautréamont walked away from his work, thereby relinquishing responsibility for it (thus leaving *Maldoror* to find eventual acclaim by the underground), then Walker's relationship to his own work has formed a similar pattern. He indicates from time to time that his voice is still unimpaired and exists as the resonant instrument that we've always known it to be – only he's been away. Where does he go? Certainly his life has proved one of the world's best-kept secrets. There are no disclosures about his private life, no sightings of his person in bars or cafés. Is he someone else in the decade in which he's uncreative? There are no confessional statements from former lovers or clues from friends as to his whereabouts. The man simply disappears and goes on disappearing. He's always away. And when he returns it's like he's made a transition through the decades with a particular set of songs and no other biographical evidence to account for his tendency to go missing.

But with the release of his masterpiece, *Tilt*, Walker agreed to doing a number of interviews that, if anything, only increased the enigma surrounding his private life. Walker, who is really Noel Scott Engel, as Lautréamont was Isidore Ducasse (both appearing pseudonymously to their public), often appears as casual about his material as Lautréamont. 'I think I said to you before,' he told an interviewer, 'I don't write until I'm ready to record. It's pointless. If I'm going to sit around in a wilderness because I can't record any songs . . . I threw a whole lot of songs away, as many as I could write. Which isn't a lot. Ever.'

Even in conversation Walker puts sunglasses on his words. And in the way that his lyrics have become increasingly pared down, each word afforded the isolation and resonance you would find in a poem by Paul Celan, so his explanations of his work are both obscure and illuminating. Of the tone of the album and his masterful delivery, he comments: 'Singing's hard for me. I've always found it difficult, but it's even harder now. I don't mean physically doing it, I mean in the sense of how it sounds, how to make it neutral. Everybody can overload it emotionally or underplay it deadpan, but to get it neutral is very hard, and that's what I'm after. It's an indecision, a grey area of vocal I want to produce.'

Walker's manner of addressing a song is usually at the blue end of the spectrum. His insurgent balladic yearning, the authority of his baritone register and the Spectorish wall of orchestral sound that accompanied his renditions of Bacharach/David tearjerkers were all pitched in a mid-blue to cobalt arena of emotions. Those moody, bluer-than-blue characteristics of his wounded sensibility only hinted at the increasing isolation that had come to invest Walker's life and work. His retreat has been that of a solitary becoming, in time, a recluse. And the older he grows, the more inseparable the life and the work appear. This was never a man adapting the role of an outsider but, rather, living it and imparting some of that deep pain to his art. Each new album is a co-extension of Walker's telescoping in on his own eventual vanishing point.

'I shall leave no memoirs,' Lautréamont tells us in his short text *Poésies*, a sentiment that I am sure would be endorsed by Walker. *Tilt* would comprise as enigmatic an autobiography as *Poésies*. Walker was prepared to offer us abstruse guidelines as to how his album came into being but omitted all reference as to why he had been compelled to write it. But even learning of his method is a disclosure we value. 'By the time I get to the studio,' he tells us, 'it's all written down. I have to have musicians I can work with, because I always want the music to be played together, at once. I don't want any drum machines or click tracks. Nothing like that. Very little overdubbing, if possible . . . I'll do a couple of tunes on the first day, then take then home and listen to them in the evening, go in and do them again if I don't like them – I don't have any equipment at home except a guitar and an amp and a little five-octave keyboard, so I don't have any fantasy or idea of what it'll be like when I get in there. So I'm surprised, constantly.'

Who are Walker's neighbours? Does anyone see him come back from a rare visit to the studio? Does anyone hear the demo tapes as he plays them in his flat? Is this all done as an act of ritual secrecy? Lautréamont, we're led to believe, had red hair. Did Isidore Ducasse dye his hair red? What I find so interesting about Walker is the way the enigmatic person behind the work translates so directly into the hermetic qualities of *Tilt*, so that there's not the slightest overlap to indicate anything about the artist's private life. Certainly the intensity of the recording, and the harrowing allusions in the songs to war, alienation and a post modern landscape from which human relations are absent, suggests the territory explored is about as close to Beckett's endgaming theatre as modern music can get. Walker has shifted his psychological terrain from subjective melancholy to universal anguish.

His obsessive fear of death or the end, something that has inveterately thumbstained his work to date, was a theme on which he was willing to speak in relation to *Tilt*: 'I don't think I've left that behind. I think I'm further into it. I felt it when I was younger in a very vertiginous kind of way, but this time it's more reconciliation, a weightier thing. I realized all the phenomena of existence very young and it was a very hard thing for me. Now I'm living with it a little easier, more as an astonishment thing than a negative thing.'

Astonishment perhaps at the realization of his being fifty-two at the time of recording *Tilt*, as opposed to forty when he recorded its equally hermetic predecessor *Climate of Hunter*. Few singers have rejected fame in the way that Walker chose to turn his back on considerable pop success in the mid- to late sixties and elected instead to direct his creative energies towards constructing a music every bit as innovative as the experimental genres established by the likes of Steve Reich, Philip Glass, Terry Riley and Brian Eno. And if the comparison seems incongruous, then I make the analogy in the light of Walker's voice having become an instrument, as we may think of Billie Holiday's voice as an instrument assimilated by her jazz accompanists.

Walker's inimitable, vibrato-drenched baritone scale of singing is used to less effect on *Tilt*, and in its place he seems to have opted for a sonorous tenor's pitch as a means of best conveying a neutral tone of singing. But there are breathtaking moments on 'Patriot (A Single)' where the voice reaches heroic proportions, the operatic thrust sounding as though Walker is keeping in check an energy that is too big to manage. And the arias that he constructs in these brief but dramatic vocal cameos in 'Patriot (A Single)' are composed around allusions to South American torturers, as in the song 'Bolivia'. 'The bad news/is there is no news,' he affirms, before the voice spectacularly alludes to the story of a deserter: 'Tonight he'll/rise/he'll leave/these arms/to anyone/who asks/about/as-in-the tracks/as-in-the wrists/as-in-you been/as-in-without.' Walker would doubtless claim that the fragmentation and obscurity of the lyrics are a part of his attempt to find in songwriting the aural equivalents of film. Incidents in the scrambled narratives that comprise the songs on *Tilt* flash by, seemingly unrelated but somehow forming an articulate and integrated texture in the overall composition. His method of writing has always tended towards the neologistic and the grammatically angular, and his emphasis tends to lie on phrases that convey a poetic rather than a literal meaning. In this particular set of lyrics he talks about having stripped the constituents of lyric to their bare components. The words in *Tilt* are horribly isolated, like prisoners awaiting torture in a concentration camp. The singer cannot protect his delivery; the words he has written return on his voice with a renewed sense of vulnerability, and the timeless process imparted to them by recording means they will remain exposed at every new listening.

What is it that makes Walker concern himself in these transpersonal songs with themes arising from South American torturers, Nazi war criminals like Eichmann and the death of the Italian film director Pier Paolo Pasolini? Or do these characters represent symbolic personae brought in to enforce the devastated inner landscape that Walker inhabits? There are no autobiographical confessions on *Tilt* and no traces of self-pity; there is only the unrelenting disquiet of genius that has, somewhere along the line, been broken.

Edmundo Montagne had been a childhood friend of Isidore Ducasse's in Montevideo, that is before Ducasse left for Paris and assumed the name Comte de Lautréamont. In an article he wrote in 1925 Montagne, who kept in touch with Isidore's father, expressed something of the mystery surrounding the young poet's death: 'I heard no mention of the *Chants*, neither then or when I grew up. All François Ducasse told me, one day, post-1875, was that Isidore had died in '70. I had always thought he'd been killed in the war.'

The mystery investing Isidore Ducasse's life and death give him the appeal of a perverse saint. We know little of how he lived and even less of how he died. In a way, he's the perfect subject for a Scott Walker song, for the two mirror each other in terms of biographical obscurity. Who was Isidore Ducasse? Who is Scott Walker? Is the latter a reincarnation of the former? Have either of them ever existed independently of the work they have given us?

The dilemma on which Walker's career has foundered is a peculiarly modern one for singers. His rise to fame in the sixties was as part of a generation that called itself singer/songwriters and that largely discredited vocalists who interpreted material written for them. That being a singer does not necessarily imply an ability to write lyrics was seen as no impediment to a new generation of pop musicians. Walker, who had begun his career as an interpretative artist, would normally have stayed in the tradition of that long line of singers whose gift was their voice and whose creativity was measured by their individual genius in colouring the lyrics. Anxious to explore his own anxiety-driven inner world, Walker, inspired by the poetic lyricism of the Belgian songwriter Jacques Brel, took to interspersing songs written by the latter with self-penned compositions on his first three solo albums. *Scott 4* was entirely self-composed, and *Til the Band Comes In* is comprised half of cover versions and half of Walker's own material. After that, he appears to have lost confidence in his songwriting abilities, and his next four solo albums all featured him in the role of reinventing other people's songs. And so the conflict raged, right through the Walker Brothers' reunion in the late seventies until his re-emergence with the masterful, self-penned *Climate of Hunter* in 1984.

But it is an agony that is little talked about. Opera singers are not required to compose librettos, so why are gifted vocalists like Walker expected to write original material? Isn't the voice sufficient as a creative instrument? Billie Holiday, Sarah Vaughan, Dusty Springfield, Peggy Lee, Shirley Bassey, Elvis Presley, Gene Pitney and Roy Orbison are all examples of singers who have relied on songwriting teams to tailor lyric and melody to their individual voices.

In Walker's case, self-composition, while it has greatly reduced his output as a singer, has allowed him to channel his creative energies into the two recondite suites of songs that comprise

Climate of Hunter and *Tilt*. Would we have liked an expansive repertoire of cover versions, with Walker singing Cole Porter, Leiber/Stoller and Charles Aznavour? Marc Almond's impassioned renditions of Aznavour's 'Yesterday When I Was Young' and 'What Makes a Man a Man' suggests that Walker could equally have applied his vocal prowess to these modern classics. His output, scarcely more than ninety minutes' music in thirteen years, is, by any standards, alarmingly unprolific. Is it lack of interest that accounts for so minimal an output, or it is a perfectionist ideal that fears failure? Is there a lack of momentum owing to the artist having renounced his past successes, thus losing the public who once bought his records? Lautréamont had almost no readers at the time of his disappearance. In his long periods of creative inertia Walker addresses the public through periodic compilation releases drawn from the more commercial phases of his work. These selections and 'Best Ofs' have something of a posthumous air about them. Where is the singer? A blond-haired Walker, photographed twenty-five years ago, stares out from the CD racks, enforcing the rumours of a death that hasn't quite happened (except in term of new material). Is there a death-pact between Walker and a bourbon bottle, or has silence become the most cherished aspect of his being? Is he listening to the empty space his voice inhabits? Walker's life is as much an open-ended fiction as Lautréamont's. In my novel *Isidore* I placed Lautréamont in a drag bar, wearing a red wig and black suspenders. What if that really happened? In my invention Lautréamont became a stripper called Isidore. Isidore or Isidora.

What is Walker doing at this moment? Is he out in Bayswater visiting the local supermarket? Nobody in the street or at the check-out point knows this person as the singer Scott Walker. His cheque card probably reads Noel Scott Engel. Voice is a concealed phenomenon. It's like a flower that opens in response to the sun. Walker's voice seems to be periodically unlocked from its subterranean depths by an inner urgency that progressively grows until it can no longer be restrained. The poet W.B. Yeats once wrote of the incredible resistance he felt to the poetic experience and how he wrote the words down only after they had come to assert a dominance that forced him to speak them out loud. In other words, the lyric impulse demanded attention. It wanted out.

I suspect Walker's inspirational guidelines operate on similar levels of breakthrough. He creates only when there is no other option and, as he points out, only when there is someone to finance his uncommercial experiments. Part of Walker's dilemma is in gauging how far out of the mainstream he can go and yet still retain a public. His following is loyal, but one suspects that his solid nucleus of admirers have remained with him from the start and have not come to *Tilt* without previous knowledge of his work. The album is more readily assimilated if we see it as part of a continuing line in his development as an artist and as an affirmation of the uncompromising integrity he has always brought to his work.

But where are we now in terms of Walker being present as a singer? In an unlikely interview with Simon Williams for the *New Musical Express*, he confessed to still being disturbed by an innate sense of self-loathing but also spoke of having come to terms with the negative aspects of his past. With his usual sense of only hinting at his private darkness, he reflected: 'Do I feel as though I did anything wrong? No, not through those times. I might have done earlier on, but I can't remember what they were because I was, uh, pretty gone. I can't remember anything. Anyway, they're a waste of time, regrets.'

Walker is undoubtedly alluding here to his alcoholism and the years he wrote off through heavy drinking. The reported earlier mismanaged suicide attempts, followed by a brief and failed marriage to Mette Teglbjaerg, seem to have been succeeded by a self-destructive impulse to drink himself into oblivion. According to Plotinus and the Neoplatonists, we forget our previous incarnation at the moment of birth and then set about retrieving what we once knew through the faculty of memory. And often it is suffering which alerts us to the need to sensitize memory. And, having opened the door, we long to close it again in order to forget. And ultimately we die in order to let go the accumulated pain of living. The same phenomenon confronts the creative artist. How much does one dare to remember? And how much to forget? Good art finds a balance between the two.

Where is Walker in this process of retrieval? *Tilt* seemed like a refusal to incorporate autobiography into the lyric texture, but hopefully the internal pressures of growing older may inspire him to record a successor to *Tilt*. 'I wouldn't write,' he explained, endeavouring to account for the lost years, 'because there was this thing whereby you had to make demos, and I can't imagine demoing any of my material. The idea is totally ridiculous. So I simply took years off.'

I imagine that no one will ever penetrate Walker's veneer and that, like Lautréamont, his life will remain an insoluble mystery. If by some weird trick of time we could bring the two together, the red-haired youth who died for his art and perversely denied us the promise of genius, and the young man who turned away from fulfilment as a singer, would they share a moment's understanding? Lautréamont used to walk through the Paris streets looking for something or someone, presumably himself. Walker is probably doing the same this moment. He is immersed in the security that comes of being anonymous in the London crowds and is simply another entity threading his way through the rainy streets of Bayswater and Queensway. What if it never really happened: the years of fame and the decades spent hiding from the deleterious effects of stardom? In his own mind he has dissociated himself from the personal confusions of a past to which he no longer belongs. But he carries a secret towards the future – the distinction of his voice. He can never be just anyone. He is always Scott Walker by virtue of his gift. When he opens the door to his apartment he faces the private arena in which he lives, puts down his shopping and listens attentively to the rain falling on his moment of being and on all who live in his adopted city.